ABOUT THIS PUBLICATION

FOR SERVICE ASSISTANCE

Customer Service Department
1.704.898.0770

North Carolina General Statues is published by The Muliti-Media Group of Greater Charlotte in Charlotte, North Carolina. Copyright 2015 by the Multi-Media Group of Greater Charlotte. This book or parts thereof may not be reproduced in any form, stored in a retrieval system, or transmitted in any form by any means—electronic, mechanical, photocopy, recording or otherwise—without prior written permission of the publisher, except as provided by United States of America copyright law.

The records required by U.S. Code 2257(a) through (c) and the pertinent regulations 28 C.F.R. Cli. 1, Part 75 with respect to this publication and all materials associated with such records are maintained by The Multi-Media Group of Greater Charlotte, Publisher and available for review by Attorney General.

www.visionbooks.org

Copyright © 2015 by MMGGC
All rights reserved!

TID: 5061411
ISBN (10) digit: 1502912902
ISBN (13) digit: 978-1502912909

123-4-56789-01239-Paperback
123-4-56789-01239-Hardback

First Edition

090520140547

Printed in the United States of America

2015 EDITION

North Carolina Criminal Law And Procedure-Pamphlet # 30

Printed In conjunction with the Administration of the Courts

North Carolina Criminal Law and Procedure
Pamphlet Reference Guide

Chapters	Pamphlet
Chapter 1 Civil Procedure	1
Chapter 1 Civil Procedure (Continue)	2
Chapter 1A Rules of Civil Procedure	2
Chapter 1B Contribution.	2
Chapter 1C Enforcement of Judgments.	2
Chapter 1D Punitive Damages.	2
Chapter 1E Eastern Band of Cherokee Indians.	2
Chapter 1F North Carolina Uniform Interstate Depositions and Discovery Act.	2
Chapter 2 - Clerk of Superior Court [Repealed and Transferred.]	3
Chapter 3 - Commissioners of Affidavits and Deeds [Repealed.]	3
Chapter 4 - Common Law	3
Chapter 5 - Contempt [Repealed.]	3
Chapter 5A - Contempt	3
Chapter 6 - Liability for Court Costs	3
Chapter 7 - Courts [Repealed and Transferred.]	3
Chapter 7A – Judicial Department	3
Chapter 7A – Continuation (Judicial Department)	4
Chapter 7A – Continuation (Judicial Department)	5
Chapter 7B - Juvenile Code	5
Chapter 8 - Evidence	6
Chapter 8A - Interpreters for Deaf Persons [Recodified.]	6
Chapter 8B - Interpreters for Deaf Persons	6
Chapter 8C - Evidence Code	6
Chapter 9 - Jurors	6
Chapter 10 - Notaries [Repealed.]	6
Chapter 10A - Notaries [Recodified.]	6
Chapter 10B - Notaries	6
Chapter 11 - Oaths	6
Chapter 12 - Statutory Construction	6
Chapter 13 - Citizenship Restored	6
Chapter 14 - Criminal Law	7
Chapter 14 –Criminal Law (Continuation)	8
Chapter 15 - Criminal Procedure	9
Chapter 15A - Criminal Procedure Act (Continuation)	10
Chapter 15A - Criminal Procedure Act (Continuation)	11
Chapter 15B - Victims Compensation	11
Chapter 15C - Address Confidentiality Program	11
Chapter 16 - Gaming Contracts and Futures	11
Chapter 17 - Habeas Corpus	11

Chapter 17A - Law-Enforcement Officers [Recodified.]	11
Chapter 17B - North Carolina Criminal Justice Education and Training System [Recodified.] Chapter 17C - North Carolina Criminal Justice Education and Training Standards Commission	11
	11
Chapter 17D - North Carolina Justice Academy	11
Chapter 17E - North Carolina Sheriffs' Education and Training Standards Commission	11
Chapter 18 - Regulation of Intoxicating Liquors [Repealed.]	12
Chapter 18A - Regulation of Intoxicating Liquors [Repealed.]	12
Chapter 18B - Regulation of Alcoholic Beverages	12
Chapter 18C - North Carolina State Lottery	12
Chapter 19 - Offenses against Public Morals	12
Chapter 19A - Protection of Animals	12
Chapter 20 - Motor Vehicles	13
Chapter 20 - Motor Vehicles (Continuation)	14
Chapter 20 - Motor Vehicles (Continuation)	15
Chapter 20 - Motor Vehicles (Continuation)	16
Chapter 21 - Bills of Lading	17
Chapter 22 - Contracts Requiring Writing	17
Chapter 22A - Signatures	17
Chapter 22B - Contracts Against Public Policy	17
Chapter 22C - Payments to Subcontractors	17
Chapter 23 - Debtor and Creditor	17
Chapter 24 – Interest	17
Chapter 25 – Uniform Commercial Code	18
Chapter 25 – Uniform Commercial Code (Continuation)	19
Chapter 25A – Retail Installment Sales Act	20
Chapter 25B - Credit	20
Chapter 25C - Sales of Artwork	20
Chapter 26 - Suretyship	20
Chapter 27 - Warehouse Receipts [Repealed.]	20
Chapter 28 - Administration [Repealed.]	20
Chapter 28A - Administration of Decedents' Estates	20
Chapter 28B - Estates of Absentees in Military Service	20
Chapter 28C - Estates of Missing Persons	20
Chapter 29 - Intestate Succession	21
Chapter 30 - Surviving Spouses	21
Chapter 31 - Wills	21
Chapter 31A - Acts Barring Property Rights	21
Chapter 31B - Renunciation of Property and Renunciation of Fiduciary Powers Act	21
Chapter 31C - Uniform Disposition of Community Property Rights at Death Act	21
Chapter 32 - Fiduciaries	21
Chapter 32A - Powers of Attorney	21
Chapter 33 - Guardian and Ward [Repealed and Recodified.]	21

Chapter 33A - North Carolina Uniform Transfers to Minors Act	21
Chapter 33B - North Carolina Uniform Custodial Trust Act	21
Chapter 34 - Veterans' Guardianship Act	22
Chapter 35 - Sterilization Procedures	22
Chapter 35A - Incompetency and Guardianship	22
Chapter 36 - Trusts and Trustees [Repealed.]	22
Chapter 36A - Trusts and Trustees	22
Chapter 36B - Uniform Management of Institutional Funds Act [Repealed.]	22
Chapter 36C - North Carolina Uniform Trust Code	22
Chapter 36D - North Carolina Community Third Party Trusts, Pooled Trusts	23
Chapter 36E - Uniform Prudent Management of Institutional Funds Act	23
Chapter 37 - Allocation of Principal and Income [Repealed.]	23
Chapter 37A - Uniform Principal and Income Act	23
Chapter 38 - Boundaries	23
Chapter 38A - Landowner Liability	23
Chapter 38B - Trespasser Responsibility	23
Chapter 39 - Conveyances	23
Chapter 39A - Transfer Fee Covenants Prohibited	23
Chapter 40 - Eminent Domain [Repealed.]	23
Chapter 40A - Eminent Domain	23
Chapter 41 - Estates	23
Chapter 41A - State Fair Housing Act	23
Chapter 42 - Landlord and Tenant	23
Chapter 42A - Vacation Rental Act	23
Chapter 43 - Land Registration	23
Chapter 44 - Liens	24
Chapter 44A - Statutory Liens and Charges	24
Chapter 45 - Mortgages and Deeds of Trust	24
Chapter 45A - Good Funds Settlement Act	24
Chapter 46 - Partition	24
Chapter 47 - Probate and Registration	25
Chapter 47A - Unit Ownership	25
Chapter 47B - Real Property Marketable Title Act	25
Chapter 47C - North Carolina Condominium Act	25
Chapter 47D - Notice of Settlement Act [Expired.]	25
Chapter 47E - Residential Property Disclosure Act	25
Chapter 47F - North Carolina Planned Community Act	25
Chapter 47G - Option to Purchase Contracts	25
Chapter 47H - Contracts for Deed	25
Chapter 48 - Adoptions +	26
Chapter 48A - Minors	26
Chapter 49 - Bastardy	26
Chapter 49A - Rights of Children	26
Chapter 50 - Divorce and Alimony	26

Chapter 50A - Uniform Child-Custody Jurisdiction and Enforcement Act	26
Chapter 50B - Domestic Violence	26
Chapter 50C - Civil No-Contact Orders	26
Chapter 51 - Marriage	26
Chapter 52 - Powers and Liabilities of Married Persons	27
Chapter 52A - Uniform Reciprocal Enforcement of Support Act [Repealed.]	27
Chapter 52B - Uniform Premarital Agreement Act	27
Chapter 52C - Uniform Interstate Family Support Act	27
Chapter 53 - Banks	27
Chapter 53A - Business Development Corporations and North Carolina Capital Resource Corporations	28
Chapter 53B - Financial Privacy Act	28
Chapter 54 - Cooperative Organizations	28
Chapter 54A - Capital Stock Savings and Loan Associations [Repealed.]	28
Chapter 54B - Savings and Loan Associations	29
Chapter 54C - Savings Banks	29
Chapter 55 - North Carolina Business Corporation Act	30
Chapter 55A - North Carolina Nonprofit Corporation Act	31
Chapter 55B - Professional Corporation Act	31
Chapter 55C - Foreign Trade Zones	31
Chapter 55D - Filings, Names, and Registered Agents for Corporations, Nonprofit Corporations, and Partnerships	31
Chapter 56 - Electric, Telegraph and Power Companies [Repealed.]	31
Chapter 57 - Hospital, Medical and Dental Service Corporations [Recodified.]	31
Chapter 57A - Health Maintenance Organization Act [Recodified.]	31
Chapter 57B - Health Maintenance Organization Act [Recodified.]	31
Chapter 57C - North Carolina Limited Liability Company Act.	31
Chapter 58 - Insurance.	32
Chapter 58 - Insurance (Continuation)	33
Chapter 58 - Insurance (Continuation)	34
Chapter 58 - Insurance (Continuation)	35
Chapter 58 - Insurance (Continuation)	36
Chapter 58 - Insurance (Continuation)	37
Chapter 58 - Insurance (Continuation)	38
Chapter 58A - North Carolina Health Insurance Trust Commission [Recodified.]	38
Chapter 59 - Partnership.	39
Chapter 59B - Uniform Unincorporated Nonprofit Association Act.	39
Chapter 60 - Railroads and Other Carriers [Repealed and Transferred.]	39
Chapter 61 - Religious Societies	39
Chapter 62 - Public Utilities	39

Chapter 62 - Public Utilities (Continuation)	40
Chapter 62A - Public Safety Telephone Service And Wireless Telephone Service	40
Chapter 63 - Aeronautics	40
Chapter 63A - North Carolina Global TransPark Authority	40
Chapter 64 - Aliens	40
Chapter 65 – Cemeteries	40
Chapter 66 - Commerce and Business	41
Chapter 67 - Dogs	41
Chapter 68 - Fences and Stock Law	41
Chapter 69 - Fire Protection	41
Chapter 70 - Indian Antiquities, Archaeological Resources and Unmarked Human Skeletal Remains Protection	42
Chapter 71 - Indians [Repealed.]	42
Chapter 71A - Indians	42
Chapter 72 - Inns, Hotels and Restaurants	42
Chapter 73 - Mills	42
Chapter 74 - Mines and Quarries	42
Chapter 74A - Company Police [Repealed.]	42
Chapter 74B - Private Protective Services Act [Repealed.]	42
Chapter 74C - Private Protective Services	42
Chapter 74D - Alarm Systems	42
Chapter 74E - Company Police Act	42
Chapter 74F - Locksmith Licensing Act	42
Chapter 74G - Campus Police Act	42
Chapter 75 - Monopolies, Trusts and Consumer Protection	42
Chapter 75A - Boating and Water Safety	43
Chapter 75B - Discrimination in Business	43
Chapter 75C - Motion Picture Fair Competition Act	43
Chapter 75D - Racketeer Influenced and Corrupt Organizations	43
Chapter 75E - Unlawful Activities in Connection With Certain Corporate Transactions	43
Chapter 76 - Navigation	43
Chapter 76A - Navigation and Pilotage Commissions	43
Chapter 77 - Rivers, Creeks, and Coastal Waters	43
Chapter 78 - Securities Law [Repealed.]	43
Chapter 78A - North Carolina Securities Act	43
Chapter 78B - Tender Offer Disclosure Act [Repealed.]	43
Chapter 78C - Investment Advisers	43
Chapter 78D - Commodities Act	43
Chapter 79 - Strays [Repealed.]	43
Chapter 80 - Trademarks, Brands, etc.	44
Chapter 81 - Weights and Measures [Recodified.]	44
Chapter 81A - Weights and Measures Act of 1975.	44
Chapter 82 - Wrecks [Repealed.]	44
Chapter 83 - Architects [Recodified.]	44

Chapter 83A - Architects	44
Chapter 84 - Attorneys-at-Law	44
Chapter 84A - Foreign Legal Consultants	44
Chapter 85 - Auctions and Auctioneers [Repealed.]	44
Chapter 85A - Bail Bondsmen and Runners [Recodified.]	44
Chapter 85B - Auctions and Auctioneers	44
Chapter 85C - Bail Bondsmen and Runners [Recodified.]	44
Chapter 86 - Barbers [Recodified.]	44
Chapter 86A - Barbers	44
Chapter 87 - Contractors	44
Chapter 88 - Cosmetic Art [Repealed.]	44
Chapter 88A - Electrolysis Practice Act	44
Chapter 88B - Cosmetic Art	45
Chapter 89 - Engineering and Land Surveying [Recodified.]	45
Chapter 89A - Landscape Architects	45
Chapter 89B - Foresters	45
Chapter 89C - Engineering and Land Surveying	45
Chapter 89D - Landscape Contractors	45
Chapter 89E - Geologists Licensing Act	45
Chapter 89F - North Carolina Soil Scientist Licensing Act	45
Chapter 89G - Irrigation Contractors	45
Chapter 90 - Medicine and Allied Occupations	45
Chapter 90 - Medicine and Allied Occupations (Continuation)	46
Chapter 90 - Medicine and Allied Occupations (Continuation)	47
Chapter 90 - Medicine and Allied Occupations (Continuation)	48
Chapter 90A - Sanitarians and Water and Wastewater Treatment Facility Operators	48
Chapter 90B - Social Worker Certification and Licensure Act	48
Chapter 90C - North Carolina Recreational Therapy Licensure Act	48
Chapter 90D - Interpreters and Transliterators	48
Chapter 91 - Pawnbrokers [Repealed.]	48
Chapter 91A - Pawnbrokers Modernization Act of 1989	48
Chapter 92 - Photographers [Deleted.]	48
Chapter 93 - Certified Public Accountants	48
Chapter 93A - Real Estate License Law	49
Chapter 93B - Occupational Licensing Boards	49
Chapter 93C - Watchmakers [Repealed.]	49
Chapter 93D - North Carolina State Hearing Aid Dealers and Fitters Board.	49
Chapter 93E - North Carolina Appraisers Act	49
Chapter 94 - Apprenticeship	49
Chapter 95 - Department of Labor and Labor Regulations	49
Chapter 95 - Department of Labor and Labor Regulations (Continuation)	50
Chapter 96 - Employment Security	50
Chapter 97 - Workers' Compensation Act	50
Chapter 97 - Workers' Compensation Act (Continuation)	51

Chapter 98 - Burnt and Lost Records	51
Chapter 99 - Libel and Slander	51
Chapter 99A - Civil Remedies for Criminal Actions	51
Chapter 99B - Products Liability	51
Chapter 99C - Actions Relating to Winter Sports Safety and Accidents	51
Chapter 99D - Civil Rights	51
Chapter 99E - Special Liability Provisions	51
Chapter 100 - Monuments, Memorials and Parks	51
Chapter 101 - Names of Persons	51
Chapter 102 - Official Survey Base	51
Chapter 103 - Sundays, Holidays and Special Days	51
Chapter 104 - United States Lands	51
Chapter 104A - Degrees of Kinship	51
Chapter 104B - Hurricanes or Other Acts of Nature	51
Chapter 104C - Atomic Energy, Radioactivity and Ionizing Radiation [Repealed and Recodified.]	51
Chapter 104D - Southern States Energy Compact	51
Chapter 104E - North Carolina Radiation Protection Act	51
Chapter 104F - Southeast Interstate Low-Level Radioactive Waste Management Compact [Repealed]	51
Chapter 104G - North Carolina Low-Level Radioactive Waste Management Authority Act of 1987 [Repealed]	51
Chapter 105 - Taxation	51
Chapter 105 - Taxation (Continuation)	52
Chapter 105 - Taxation (Continuation)	53
Chapter 105 - Taxation (Continuation)	54
Chapter 105A - Setoff Debt Collection Act	55
Chapter 105B - Defaulted Student Loan Recovery Act	55
Chapter 106 - Agriculture	55
Chapter 106 - Agriculture (Continue)	56
Chapter 106 - Agriculture (Continue)	57
Chapter 107 - Agricultural Development Districts [Repealed.]	57
Chapter 108 - Social Services [Repealed and Recodified.]	57
Chapter 108A - Social Services	57
Chapter 108B - Community Action Programs	58
Chapter 108C Medicaid and Health Choice Provider Requirements.	58
Chapter 108D Medicaid Managed Care for Behavioral Health Services.	58
Chapter 109 - Bonds [Recodified.]	58
Chapter 110 - Child Welfare	58
Chapter 111 - Aid to the Blind	58
Chapter 112 - Confederate Homes and Pensions [Repealed.]	58
Chapter 113 - Conservation and Development	58
Chapter 113 - Conservation and Development (Continuation)	59

Chapter 113A - Pollution Control and Environment	59
Chapter 113A - Pollution Control and Environment (Continuation)	60
Chapter 113B - North Carolina Energy Policy Act of 1975	60
Chapter 114 - Department of Justice	60
Chapter 115 - Elementary and Secondary Education [Repealed.]	60
Chapter 115A - Community Colleges, Technical Institutes, and Industrial Education Centers [Repealed.]	60
Chapter 115B - Tuition and Fee Waivers	60
Chapter 115C - Elementary and Secondary Education	60
Chapter 115C - Elementary and Secondary Education (Continuation)	61
Chapter 115C - Elementary and Secondary Education (Continuation)	62
Chapter 115C - Elementary and Secondary Education (Continuation)	63
Chapter 115D - Community Colleges	63
Chapter 115E - Private Educational Facilities Finance Act [Recodified]	63
Chapter 116 - Higher Education	63
Chapter 116 - Higher Education (Continuation)	63
Chapter 116A - Escheats and Abandoned Property [Repealed.]	64
Chapter 116B - Escheats and Abandoned Property	64
Chapter 116C - Continuum of Education Programs	64
Chapter 116D - Higher Education Bonds	64
Chapter 117 - Electrification	64
Chapter 118 - Firemen's and Rescue Squad Workers' Relief and Pension Funds [Recodified.]	64
Chapter 118A - Firemen's Death Benefit Act [Repealed.]	64
Chapter 118B - Members of a Rescue Squad Death Benefit Act [Repealed.]	64
Chapter 119 - Gasoline and Oil Inspection and Regulation	64
Chapter 120 - General Assembly	65
Chapter 120 - General Assembly (Continuation)	66
Chapter 120 - General Assembly (Continuation)	67
Chapter 120C - Lobbying	67
Chapter 121 - Archives and History	67
Chapter 122 - Hospitals for the Mentally Disordered [Repealed.]	67
Chapter 122A - North Carolina Housing Finance Agency	67
Chapter 122B - North Carolina Agricultural Facilities Finance Act [Repealed.]	67
Chapter 122C - Mental Health, Developmental Disabilities, and Substance Abuse Act of 1985	67
Chapter 122C - Mental Health, Developmental Disabilities, and Substance Abuse Act of 1985 (Continuation)	68
Chapter 122D - North Carolina Agricultural Finance Act	68

Chapter 122E - North Carolina Housing Trust and Oil Overcharge Act	68
Chapter 123 - Impeachment	69
Chapter 123A - Industrial Development [Repealed.]	69
Chapter 124 - Internal Improvements	69
Chapter 125 - Libraries	69
Chapter 126 - State Personnel System	69
Chapter 127 - Militia [Repealed.]	69
Chapter 127A - Militia	69
Chapter 127B - Military Affairs	69
Chapter 127C - Advisory Commission on Military Affairs	69
Chapter 128 - Offices and Public Officers	69
Chapter 128 - Offices and Public Officers (Continuation)	70
Chapter 129 - Public Buildings and Grounds	70
Chapter 130 - Public Health [Repealed.]	70
Chapter 130A - Public Health	70
Chapter 130A - Public Health (Continuation)	71
Chapter 130A - Public Health (Continuation)	72
Chapter 130B - Hazardous Waste Management Commission [Repealed.]	72
Chapter 131 - Public Hospitals [Repealed.]	72
Chapter 131A - Health Care Facilities Finance Act	72
Chapter 131B - Licensing of Ambulatory Surgical Facilities [Repealed.]	72
Chapter 131C - Charitable Solicitation Licensure Act [Repealed.]	72
Chapter 131D - Inspection and Licensing of Facilities	72
Chapter 131E - Health Care Facilities and Services	72
Chapter 131E - Health Care Facilities and Services (Continuation)	73
Chapter 131F - Solicitation of Contributions	73
Chapter 132 - Public Records	73
Chapter 133 - Public Works	74
Chapter 134 - Youth Development [Recodified.]	74
Chapter 134A - Youth Services [Repealed.]	74
Chapter 135 - Retirement System for Teachers and State Employees; Social Security; Health Insurance Program for Children	74
Chapter 135 - Retirement System for Teachers and State Employees; Social Security; Health Insurance Program for Children	75
Chapter 136 - Transportation	75
Chapter 136 - Transportation (Continuation)	76
Chapter 137 - Rural Rehabilitation [Repealed.]	76
Chapter 138 - Salaries, Fees and Allowances	76
Chapter 138A - State Government Ethics Act	76
Chapter 139 - Soil and Water Conservation Districts	76

Chapter 140 - State Art Museum; Symphony and Art Societies	76
Chapter 140A - State Awards System	76
Chapter 141 - State Boundaries	76
Chapter 142 - State Debt	76
Chapter 143 - State Departments, Institutions, and Commissions	77
Chapter 143 - State Departments, Institutions, and Commissions (Continuation)	78
Chapter 143 - State Departments, Institutions, and Commissions (Continuation)	79
Chapter 143 - State Departments, Institutions, and Commissions (Continuation)	80
Chapter 143A - State Government Reorganization	80
Chapter 143B - Executive Organization Act of 1973	80
Chapter 143B - Executive Organization Act of 1973 (Continuation)	81
Chapter 143B - Executive Organization Act of 1973 (Continuation)	82
Chapter 143C - State Budget Act	83
Chapter 143D - The State Governmental Accountability and Internal Control Act	83
Chapter 144 - State Flag, Official Governmental Flags, Motto, and Colors	83
Chapter 145 - State Symbols and Other Official Adoptions.	83
Chapter 146 - State Lands	83
Chapter 147 - State Officers	83
Chapter 148 - State Prison System	84
Chapter 149 - State Song and Toast	84
Chapter 150 - Uniform Revocation of Licenses [Repealed.]	84
Chapter 150A - Administrative Procedure Act [Recodified.]	84
Chapter 150B - Administrative Procedure Act	84
Chapter 151 - Constables [Repealed.]	84
Chapter 152 - Coroners	84
Chapter 152A - County Medical Examiner [Repealed.]	84
Chapter 152A - County Medical Examiner [Repealed.] (Continuation)	85
Chapter 153 - Counties and County Commissioners [Repealed.]	85
Chapter 153A - Counties	85
Chapter 153B - Mountain Resources Planning Act	85
Chapter 153C - Uwharrie Regional Resources Act	85
Chapter 154 - County Surveyor [Repealed.]	85
Chapter 155 - County Treasurer [Repealed.]	85
Chapter 156 - Drainage	85
Chapter 156 – Drainage (Continuation)	86

Chapter 157 - Housing Authorities and Projects	86
Chapter 157A - Historic Properties Commissions [Transferred.]	86
Chapter 158 - Local Development	86
Chapter 159 - Local Government Finance	86
Chapter 159 - Local Government Finance (Continuation)	87
Chapter 159A - Pollution Abatement and Industrial Facilities Financing Act [Unconstitutional.]	87
Chapter 159B - Joint Municipal Electric Power and Energy Act	87
Chapter 159C - Industrial and Pollution Control Facilities Financing Act	87
Chapter 159D - The North Carolina Capital Facilities Financing Act	87
Chapter 159E - Registered Public Obligations Act	87
Chapter 159F - North Carolina Energy Development Authority [Repealed.]	87
Chapter 159G - Water Infrastructure	87
Chapter 159H - [Reserved.]	87
Chapter 159I - Solid Waste Management Loan Program and Local Government Special Obligation Bonds	87
Chapter 160 - Municipal Corporations [Repealed And Transferred.]	87
Chapter 160A - Cities and Towns	88
Chapter 160A - Cities and Towns (Continuation)	89
Chapter 160B - Consolidated City-County Act	89
Chapter 160C - Baseball Park Districts [Repealed.]	90
Chapter 161 - Register of Deeds	90
Chapter 162 - Sheriff	90
Chapter 162A - Water and Sewer Systems	90
Chapter 162B Continuity of Local Government in Emergency.	90
Chapter 163 Elections and Election Laws.	90
Chapter 163 Elections and Election Laws. (Continuation)	91
Chapter 164 Concerning the General Statutes of North Carolina.	92
Chapter 165 Veterans.	92
Chapter 166 Civil Preparedness Agencies [Repealed.]	92
Chapter 166A North Carolina Emergency Management Act.	92
Chapter 167 State Civil Air Patrol [Repealed.]	92
Chapter 168 Persons with Disabilities.	92
Chapter 168A Persons With Disabilities Protection Act.	92

Chapter 55

North Carolina Business Corporation Act.

Article 1.

General Provisions.

Part 1. Short Title and Reservation of Power.

§ 55-1-01. Short title.

This Chapter shall be known and may be cited as the "North Carolina Business Corporation Act". (1955, c. 1371, s. 1; 1989, c. 265, s. 1.)

§ 55-1-02. Reservation of power to amend or repeal.

The General Assembly has power to amend or repeal all or part of this Chapter at any time and all domestic and foreign corporations subject to this Chapter are governed by the amendment or repeal. (1901, c. 2, s. 7; Rev., s. 1136; C.S., s. 1135; G.S. 55-36; 1955, c. 1371, s. 1; 1989, c. 265, s. 1.)

§§ 55-1-03 through 55-1-19. Reserved for future codification purposes.

Part 2. Filing Documents.

§ 55-1-20. Filing requirements.

(a)   A document required or permitted by this Chapter to be filed by the Secretary of State must be filed under Chapter 55D of the General Statutes.

(b)   A document submitted on behalf of a domestic or foreign corporation must be executed:

(1) By the chair of its board of directors, by its president, or by another of its officers;

(2) If directors have not been selected or the corporation has not been formed, by an incorporator; or

(3) If the corporation is in the hands of a receiver, trustee, or other court-appointed fiduciary, by that fiduciary.

(c) through (i). Reserved.

(j) Repealed by Session Laws 2002-159, s. 15 effective October 11, 2002. (1955, c. 1371, s. 1; 1967, c. 13, s. 1; c. 823, s. 16; 1989, c. 265, s. 1; 1989 (Reg. Sess., 1990), c. 1024, s. 12.1(a); 1991, c. 645, s. 15; 1999-369, s. 1.1; 2001-358, ss. 3(a), 6(a); 2001-387, ss. 1, 155, 173; 2001-413, s. 6; 2002-159, s. 15.)

§ 55-1-21. Forms.

(a) The Secretary of State may promulgate and furnish on request forms for the following:

(1) An application for a certificate of existence.

(2) A foreign corporation's application for a certificate of authority to transact business in this State.

(3) A foreign corporation's application for a certificate of withdrawal.

(4) Repealed by Session Laws 1997-475, s. 6.2.

If the Secretary of State so requires, use of these forms is mandatory.

(b) The Secretary of State may promulgate and furnish on request forms for other documents required or permitted to be filed by this Chapter but their use is not mandatory. (1955, c. 1371, s. 1; 1989, c. 265, s. 1; 1997-475, s. 6.2.)

§ 55-1-22. Filing, service, and copying fees.

(a) The Secretary of State shall collect the following fees when the documents described in this subsection are delivered to the Secretary for filing:

    Document
Fee

(1)   Articles of incorporation
$125.00

(2)   Application for reserved name
30.00

(3)   Notice of transfer of reserved name
10.00

(4)   Application for registered name
10.00

(5)   Application for renewal of registered name
10.00

(6)   Corporation's statement of change of registered agent or registered

    office or both
5.00

(7)   Agent's statement of change of registered office for each affected

    corporation
5.00

(8)   Agent's statement of resignation
No fee

(9)   Designation of registered agent or registered office or both
5.00

(10)   Amendment of articles of incorporation
50.00

(11) Restated articles of incorporation
10.00

with amendment of articles
50.00

(12) Articles of merger or share exchange
50.00

(12a) Articles of conversion (other than articles of conversion included as

part of another document)
50.00

(13) Articles of dissolution
30.00

(14) Articles of revocation of dissolution
10.00

(15) Certificate of administrative dissolution
No fee

(16) Application for reinstatement following administrative dissolution
100.00

(17) Certificate of reinstatement
No fee

(18) Certificate of judicial dissolution
No fee

(19) Application for certificate of authority
250.00

(20) Application for amended certificate of authority
75.00

(21) Application for certificate of withdrawal
25.00

(22) Certificate of revocation of authority to transact business
No fee

(23) Annual report (paper)
25.00

(23a) Annual report (electronic)
18.00

(24) Articles of correction
10.00

(25) Application for certificate of existence or authorization (paper)
15.00

(25a) Application for certificate of existence or authorization (electronic)
10.00

(26) Any other document required or permitted to be filed by this Chapter
10.00

(27) Repealed by Session Laws 2001-358, s. 6(b), effective January 1, 2002.

(b) The Secretary of State shall collect a fee of ten dollars ($10.00) each time process is served on the Secretary under this Chapter. The party to a proceeding causing service of process is entitled to recover this fee as costs if the party prevails in the proceeding.

(c) The Secretary of State shall collect the following fees for copying, comparing, and certifying a copy of any filed document relating to a domestic or foreign corporation:

(1) One dollar ($1.00) a page for copying or comparing a copy to the original.

(2) Fifteen dollars ($15.00) for a paper certificate.

(3) Ten dollars ($10.00) for an electronic certificate.

(d) The fee for the annual report in subdivision (23) of this section is nonrefundable. (1957, c. 1180; 1967, c. 823, s. 20; 1969, c. 751, ss. 42, 43, 45; c. 797, ss. 4, 5; 1975, 2nd Sess., c. 981, s. 1; 1983, c. 713, ss. 32-38; 1989, c. 265, s. 1; c. 714; 1989 (Reg. Sess., 1990), c. 1057; 1991, c. 574, s. 1; 1997-456, s. 55.3; 1997-475, s. 5.1; 1997-485, s. 10; 2001-358, s. 6(b); 2001-387, ss. 2, 173; 2001-413, s. 6; 2002-126, ss. 29A.25, 29A.26; 2003-349, s. 7; 2007-323, s. 30.6(a).)

§§ 55-1-22.1 through 55-1-27: Transferred to §§ 55D-11 through 55D-17 by Session Laws 2001-358, s. 3(b).

§ 55-1-28. Certificate of existence.

(a) Anyone may apply to the Secretary of State to furnish a certificate of existence for a domestic corporation or a certificate of authorization for a foreign corporation.

(b) A certificate of existence or authorization sets forth:

(1) The domestic corporation's corporate name or the foreign corporation's corporate name used in this State;

(2) That (i) the domestic corporation is duly incorporated under the law of this State, the date of its incorporation, and the period of its duration if less than perpetual; or (ii) that the foreign corporation is authorized to transact business in this State;

(3) That the articles of incorporation of a domestic corporation or the certificate of authority of a foreign corporation has not been suspended for failure to comply with the Revenue Act of this State and that the corporation has not been administratively dissolved for failure to comply with the provisions of this Chapter;

(4) That its most recent annual report required by G.S. 55-16-22 either has been delivered to the Secretary of State or is not delinquent;

(5) That articles of dissolution have not been filed; and

(6) Other facts of record in the office of the Secretary of State that may be requested by the applicant.

(c) Subject to any qualification stated in the certificate, a certificate of existence or authorization issued by the Secretary of State may be relied upon as conclusive evidence that the domestic or foreign corporation is in existence or is authorized to transact business in this State. (1955, c. 1371, s. 1; 1989, c. 265, s. 1; 1991, c. 645, s. 1; 1997-475, s. 6.3.)

§ 55-1-29: Transferred to § 55D-18 by Session Laws 2001-358, s. 3(b).

Part 3. Secretary of State.

§ 55-1-30. Powers.

The Secretary of State has the power reasonably necessary to perform the duties required of him by this Chapter. (1955, c. 1371, s. 1; 1989, c. 265, s. 1.)

§ 55-1-31. Interrogatories by Secretary of State.

The Secretary of State may propound to any corporation, domestic or foreign which he has reason to believe is subject to the provisions of this Chapter, and to any officer or director thereof, such written interrogatories as may be reasonably necessary and proper to enable him to ascertain whether such corporation is subject to the provisions of this Chapter or has complied with all the provisions of this Chapter applicable to it. Subject to applicable jurisdictional requirements, such interrogatories shall be answered within 30 days after the mailing therefor, or within such additional time as shall be fixed by the Secretary of State, and the answers thereto shall be full and complete and shall be made in writing and under oath. If such interrogatories be directed to an individual they shall be answered by him, and if directed to a corporation they shall be answered by the president, vice-president, secretary or assistant secretary thereof. The Secretary of State shall certify to the Attorney General, for such action as the Attorney General may deem appropriate, all interrogatories and answers thereto which disclose a violation of any of the provisions of this Chapter, requiring or permitting action by the Attorney General. (1955, c. 1371, s. 1; 1989, c. 265, s. 1.)

§ 55-1-32. Penalties imposed upon corporations, officers, and directors for failure to answer interrogatories.

(a) The knowing failure or refusal of a domestic or foreign corporation to answer truthfully and fully within the time prescribed in this Chapter interrogatories propounded by the Secretary of State in accordance with the provisions of this Chapter shall constitute grounds for administrative dissolution under G.S. 55-14-20 or for revocation under G.S. 55-15-30, as the case may be.

(b) Each officer and director of a domestic or foreign corporation who knowingly fails or refuses within the time prescribed by this Chapter to answer truthfully and fully interrogatories propounded to him by the Secretary of State in accordance with the provisions of this Chapter shall be guilty of a Class 1 misdemeanor. (1955, c. 1371, s. 1; 1989, c. 265, s. 1; 1993, c. 539, s. 440, c. 552, s. 3; 1994, Ex. Sess., c. 24, s. 14(c).)

§ 55-1-33. Information disclosed by interrogatories.

Interrogatories propounded by the Secretary of State and the answers thereto shall not be open to public inspection nor shall the Secretary of State disclose any facts or information obtained therefrom except insofar as his official duty may require the same to be made public or in the event such interrogatories or the answers thereto are required for evidence in any criminal proceedings or in any other action or proceedings by this State. (1955, c. 1371, s. 1; 1989, c. 265, s. 1.)

§§ 55-1-34 through 55-1-39. Reserved for future codification purposes.

Part 4. Definitions.

§ 55-1-40. Chapter definitions.

In this Chapter unless otherwise specifically provided:

(1)   "Articles of incorporation" include amended and restated articles of incorporation and articles of merger.

(2)   "Authorized shares" means the shares of all classes a domestic or foreign corporation is authorized to issue.

(2a)   "Business entity," as used in G.S. 55-11-10 and Article 11A of this Chapter, means a domestic corporation (including a professional corporation as defined in G.S. 55B-2), a foreign corporation, a domestic or foreign nonprofit corporation, a domestic or foreign limited liability company, a domestic or foreign limited partnership, a registered limited liability partnership or foreign limited liability partnership as defined in G.S. 59-32, or any other partnership as defined in G.S. 59-36 whether or not formed under the laws of this State.

(3)   "Conspicuous" means so written that a reasonable person against whom the writing is to operate should have noticed it. For example, printing in italics or boldface or contrasting color, or typing in capitals or underlined, is conspicuous.

(4)   "Corporation" or "domestic corporation" means a corporation for profit or a corporation having capital stock that is incorporated under or subject to the provisions of this Chapter and that is not a foreign corporation except that in G.S. 55-9-01 and G.S. 55-15-21 "corporation" includes domestic and foreign corporations.

(5)   "Deliver" includes mail.

(6)   "Distribution" means a direct or indirect transfer of money or other property (except its own shares) or incurrence of indebtedness by a corporation to or for the benefit of its shareholders in respect of any of its shares. A distribution may be in the form of a declaration or payment of a dividend; a purchase, redemption, or other acquisition of shares; a distribution of indebtedness; or otherwise.

(6a)   "Dividend credit" as used in G.S. 55-6-01(d)(5) means the aggregate of all yearly dividend credits. "Yearly dividend credit" means with respect to noncumulative preferred shares, the amount by which the full dividend preference of such a share, to the extent that such preference is earned by the corporation with respect to such a share in a particular fiscal year, exceeds the dividends paid on said share for that year; provided, that no dividend credit shall accrue unless, and only to the extent that, there exists an earned surplus at the end of such fiscal year. Computations of earnings allocable to classes of shares made in good faith by the board of directors in accordance with generally accepted accounting principles shall be conclusive. For the purpose of this definition, a dividend is deemed paid if it has been declared and funds for its payment have been set aside.

(6b) "Domestic limited liability company" has the same meaning as the term "LLC" in G.S. 57D-1-03.

(6c) "Domestic limited partnership" has the same meaning as in G.S. 59-102.

(6d) "Domestic nonprofit corporation" means a corporation as defined in G.S. 55A-1-40.

(7) "Effective date of notice" is defined in G.S. 55-1-41.

(8) "Electronic" has the same meaning as in G.S. 66-312.

(8a) "Electronic record" has the same meaning as in G.S. 66-312.

(8b) "Electronic signature" has the same meaning as in G.S. 66-312.

(9) "Entity" includes (without limiting the meaning of such term in Article 9 of this Chapter):

a. Any domestic or foreign:

1. Corporation; nonprofit corporation; professional corporation;

2. Limited liability company;

3. Profit and nonprofit unincorporated association; and

4. Business trust, estate, partnership, trust;

b. Two or more persons having a joint or common economic interest; and

c. The United States, and any state and foreign government.

(10) "Foreign corporation" means a corporation for profit incorporated under a law other than the law of this State.

(10a) "Foreign limited liability company" has the same meaning as the term "foreign LLC" in G.S. 57D-1-03.

(10b) "Foreign limited partnership" has the same meaning as in G.S. 59-102.

(10c) "Foreign nonprofit corporation" means a foreign corporation as defined in G.S. 55A-1-40.

(11) "Governmental subdivision" includes authority, county, district, and municipality.

(12) "Includes" means a partial definition.

(13) "Individual" denotes a natural person legally competent to act and also includes the estate of an incompetent or deceased individual.

(13a) An item is "mailed" when it is deposited in the United States mail with postage thereon prepaid and correctly addressed. When a corporation mails an item to a shareholder, "correctly addressed" means addressed to the shareholder's address as shown in the corporation's current record of shareholders.

(14) "Means" denotes an exhaustive definition.

(14a) "Merger" as used in Article 9 includes a "share exchange" as used in Article 11.

(15) "Notice" includes demand and is defined in G.S. 55-1-41.

(16) "Person" includes individual and entity.

(17) "Principal office" means the office (in or out of this State) where the principal executive offices of a domestic or foreign corporation are located, as designated in its most recent annual report filed with the Secretary of State or, in the case of a domestic or foreign corporation that has not yet filed an annual

report, in its articles of incorporation or application for a certificate of authority, respectively.

(18) "Proceeding" includes civil suit and criminal, administrative, and investigatory action.

(18a) "Public corporation" means any corporation that has a class of shares registered under Section 12 of the Securities Exchange Act of 1934, as amended (15 U.S.C. § 78l).

(19) "Record date" means the date established under Article 6 or 7 on which a corporation determines the identity of its shareholders for purposes of this Chapter.

(20) "Secretary" means the corporate officer to whom the board of directors has delegated responsibility under G.S. 55-8-40(c) for custody of the minutes of the meetings of the board of directors and of the shareholders and for authenticating records of the corporation.

(21) "Shares" means the units into which the proprietary interests in a corporation are divided.

(22) "Shareholder" means the person in whose name shares are registered in the records of a corporation or the beneficial owner of shares to the extent of the rights granted by a nominee certificate on file with a corporation.

(23) "State", when referring to a part of the United States, includes a state and commonwealth (and their agencies and governmental subdivisions) and a territory and insular possession (and their agencies and governmental subdivisions) of the United States.

(24) "Subscriber" means a person who subscribes for shares in a corporation, whether before or after incorporation.

(24a) "Unincorporated entity" means a domestic or foreign limited liability company, a domestic or foreign limited partnership, a registered limited liability partnership or foreign limited liability partnership as defined in G.S. 59-32, or any other partnership as defined in G.S. 59-36, whether or not formed under the laws of this State.

(25) "United States" includes district, authority, bureau, commission, department, and any other agency of the United States.

(26) "Voting group" means all shares of one or more classes or series that under the articles of incorporation or this Chapter are entitled to vote and be counted together collectively on a matter at a meeting of shareholders. All shares entitled by the articles of incorporation or this Chapter to vote generally on the matter are for that purpose a single voting group. (1955, c. 1371, s. 1; 1959, c. 1316, s. 1; 1989, c. 265, s. 1; 1989 (Reg. Sess., 1990), c. 1024, s. 12.4; 1993, c. 552, s. 4; 1999-369, ss. 1.2, 1.3; 1999-456, s. 3; 2001-358, s. 5(a); 2001-387, ss. 3, 4, 5, 173, 175(a); 2001-413, s. 6; 2001-487, s. 62(a); 2013-157, s. 3.)

§ 55-1-41. Notice.

(a) Notice under this Chapter shall be in writing unless oral notice is authorized in the corporation's articles of incorporation or bylaws and written notice is not specifically required by this Chapter.

(b) Notice may be communicated in person; by electronic means; or by mail or private carrier. If these forms of personal notice are impracticable as to one or more persons, notice may be communicated to such persons by publishing notice in a newspaper in the county wherein the corporation has its principal place of business in the State, or if it has no principal place of business in the State, the county wherein it has its registered office; or by radio, television, or other form of public broadcast communication.

(c) Written notice by a domestic or foreign corporation to its shareholder is effective when deposited in the United States mail with postage thereon prepaid and correctly addressed to the shareholder's address shown in the corporation's current record of shareholders. To the extent the corporation pursuant to G.S. 55-1-50 and the shareholder have agreed, notice by a domestic corporation to its shareholder in the form of an electronic record sent by electronic means is effective when it is sent as provided in G.S. 66-325. A shareholder may terminate any such agreement at any time on a prospective basis effective upon written notice of termination to the corporation or upon such later date as may be specified in the notice.

(d) Written notice to a domestic or foreign corporation (authorized to transact business in this State) may be addressed to its registered agent at its registered office or to the corporation or its secretary at its principal office shown in its most recent annual report on file in the office of the Secretary of State or, in the case of a domestic or foreign corporation that has not yet filed an annual report, in its articles of incorporation or application for a certificate of authority, respectively.

(e) Except as provided in subsection (c), written notice is effective at the earliest of the following:

(1) When received;

(2) Five days after its deposit in the United States mail, as evidenced by the postmark or otherwise, if mailed with at least first-class postage thereon prepaid and correctly addressed;

(3) On the date shown on the return receipt, if sent by registered or certified mail, return receipt requested, and the receipt is signed by or on behalf of the addressee.

In the case of notice in the form of an electronic record sent by electronic means, the time of receipt shall be determined as provided in G.S. 66-325.

(f) Oral notice is effective when actually communicated to the person entitled thereto.

(g) If this Chapter prescribes notice requirements for particular circumstances, those requirements govern. If articles of incorporation or bylaws prescribe notice requirements not inconsistent with this section or other provisions of this Chapter, those requirements govern. (1989, c. 265, s. 1; 1993, c. 552, s. 5; 2001-387, s. 6.)

§ 55-1-42. Number of shareholders.

(a) For purposes of this Chapter, the following identified as a shareholder in a corporation's current record of shareholders constitutes one shareholder:

(1) All co-owners of the same shares;

(2) A corporation, partnership, trust, estate, or other entity;

(3) The trustees, guardians, custodians, or other fiduciaries of a single trust, estate, or account.

(b) For purposes of this Chapter, shareholdings registered in substantially similar names constitute one shareholder if it is reasonable to believe that the names represent the same person. (1989, c. 265, s. 1.)

§§ 55-1-43 through 55-1-49. Reserved for future codification purposes.

Part 5. Miscellaneous.

§ 55-1-50. Electronic transactions.

For purposes of applying Article 40 of Chapter 66 of the General Statutes to transactions under this Chapter, a corporation may agree to conduct a transaction by electronic means through provision in its articles of incorporation or bylaws or by action of its board of directors. (2001-387, s. 7.)

Article 2.

Incorporation.

§ 55-2-01. Incorporators.

One or more persons may act as the incorporator or incorporators of a corporation by delivering articles of incorporation to the Secretary of State for filing. (Code, ss. 677, 678, 679, 682; 1885, cc. 19, 190; 1893, c. 318; 1897, c. 204; 1901, c. 2, ss. 8, 9; cc. 6, 41; 1903, c. 453; Rev., ss. 1137, 1139; C.S., s. 1114; 1945, c. 635; G.S., ss. 55-2, 55-3; 1951, c. 265, s. 1; 1955, c. 1371, s. 1; 1969, c. 751, s. 1; 1971, c. 1231, s. 1; 1989, c. 265, s. 1.)

§ 55-2-02. Articles of incorporation.

(a) The articles of incorporation must set forth:

(1) A corporate name for the corporation that satisfies the requirements of G.S. 55D-20 and G.S. 55D-21;

(2) The number of shares the corporation is authorized to issue and any other information required by G.S. 55-6-01;

(3) The street address, and the mailing address if different from the street address, of the corporation's initial registered office, the county in which the initial registered office is located, and the name of the corporation's initial registered agent at that address;

(3a) The street address, and the mailing address if different from the street address, of the corporation's principal office, if any, and the county in which the principal office, if any, is located; and

(4) The name and address of each incorporator.

(b) The articles of incorporation may set forth any provision that under this Chapter is required or permitted to be set forth in the bylaws, and may also set forth:

(1) The names and addresses of the individuals who are to serve as the initial directors;

(2) Provisions not inconsistent with law regarding (i) the purpose or purposes for which the corporation is organized; (ii) managing the business and regulating the affairs of the corporation; (iii) defining, limiting, and regulating the powers of the corporation, its board of directors, and shareholders; (iv) a par value for authorized shares or classes of shares; (v) the imposition of personal liability on shareholders for the debts of the corporation to a specified extent and upon specified conditions; (vi) any limitation on the duration of the corporation; and

(3) A provision limiting or eliminating the personal liability of any director arising out of an action whether by or in the right of the corporation or otherwise

for monetary damages for breach of any duty as a director. No such provision shall be effective with respect to (i) acts or omissions that the director at the time of such breach knew or believed were clearly in conflict with the best interests of the corporation, (ii) any liability under G.S. 55-8-33, (iii) any transaction from which the director derived an improper personal benefit, or (iv) acts or omissions occurring prior to the date the provisions became effective. As used herein, the term "improper personal benefit" does not include a director's reasonable compensation or other reasonable incidental benefit for or on account of his service as a director, officer, employee, independent contractor, attorney, or consultant of the corporation. A provision permitted by this Chapter in the articles of incorporation, bylaws, or a contract or resolution indemnifying or agreeing to indemnify a director against personal liability shall be fully effective whether or not there is a provision in the articles of incorporation limiting or eliminating personal liability.

(c)   The articles of incorporation need not set forth any of the corporate powers enumerated in this Chapter.

(d)   Articles of incorporation filed to effect the conversion of another business entity pursuant to Article 11A of this Chapter shall also include the statements required by G.S. 55-11A-03(a). (Code, s. 677; 1885, c. 19; 1889, c. 170; 1891, c. 257; 1893, c. 244; 1901, c. 2, s. 8; c. 47; 1903, c. 453; Rev., s. 1137; 1911, c. 213, s. 1; 1913, c. 5, s. 1; C.S., s. 1114; Ex. Sess. 1920, c. 55; 1924, c. 98; 1935, cc. 166, 320; 1939, c. 222; G.S., s. 55-2; 1951, c. 265, s. 1; 1955, c. 1371, s. 1; 1957, c. 979, s. 5; 1959, c. 1316, s. 11/2; 1969, c. 751, s. 2; 1973, c. 469, s. 2; 1987, c. 626, s. 1; 1989, c. 265, s. 1; 1993, c. 552, s. 6; 2001-358, s. 16; 2001-387, ss. 8, 9, 173, 175(a); 2001-413, s. 6.)

§ 55-2-03. Incorporation.

(a)   Corporate existence begins when the articles of incorporation become effective.

(b)   The Secretary of State's filing of the articles of incorporation is conclusive proof that the incorporators satisfied all conditions precedent to incorporation except in a proceeding by the State to cancel or revoke the incorporation or involuntarily dissolve the corporation.

(c)   No provision in this Chapter or any prior act shall be construed to require that a corporation have more than one shareholder. (1901, c. 2, s. 10; Rev., s. 1140; C.S., s. 1116; G.S., s. 55-4; 1955, c. 1371, s. 1; 1957, c. 550, ss. 2, 3; 1967, c. 13, s. 3; 1989, c. 265, s. 1; 2001-387, s. 10.)

§ 55-2-04. Reserved for future codification purposes.

§ 55-2-05. Organization of corporation.

(a)   After incorporation:

(1)   If initial directors are named in the articles of incorporation, the initial directors shall hold an organizational meeting at the call of a majority of the directors to complete the organization of the corporation by appointing officers, adopting bylaws, and carrying on any other business brought before the meeting;

(2)   If initial directors are not named in the articles, the incorporator or incorporators shall hold an organizational meeting at the call of a majority of the incorporators: (i) to elect directors and complete the organization of the corporation; or (ii) to elect a board of directors who shall complete the organization of the corporation.

(b)   Action required or permitted by this Chapter to be taken by incorporators at an organizational meeting may be taken without a meeting if the action taken is evidenced by one or more written consents describing the action taken and signed by each incorporator. If the incorporators act at a meeting, the notice and procedural provisions of G.S. 55-8-22, 55-8-23, and 55-8-24 shall apply.

(c)   An organizational meeting may be held in or out of this State. (Code, s. 665; 1901, c. 2, s. 18; Rev., s. 1142; C.S., s. 1118; G.S., s. 55-6; 1955, c. 1371, s. 1; 1969, c. 751, s. 3; 1989, c. 265, s. 1.)

§ 55-2-06. Bylaws.

(a) The incorporators or board of directors of a corporation shall adopt initial bylaws for the corporation.

(b) The bylaws of a corporation may contain any provision for managing the business and regulating the affairs of the corporation that is not inconsistent with law or the articles of incorporation. (1955, c. 1371, s. 1; 1959, c. 1316, ss. 2, 3; 1973, c. 469, s. 4; 1989, c. 265, s. 1.)

§ 55-2-07. Emergency bylaws.

(a) Unless the articles of incorporation provide otherwise, the board of directors of a corporation may adopt bylaws to be effective only in an emergency defined in subsection (d). The emergency bylaws, which are subject to amendment or repeal by the shareholders, may make all provisions necessary for managing the corporation during the emergency, including:

(1) Procedures for calling a meeting of the board of directors;

(2) Quorum requirements for the meeting; and

(3) Designation of additional or substitute directors.

(b) All provisions of the regular bylaws consistent with the emergency bylaws remain effective during the emergency. The emergency bylaws are not effective after the emergency ends.

(c) Corporate action taken in good faith in accordance with the emergency bylaws binds the corporation and the fact that the action was taken by special procedures may not be used to impose liability on a corporate director, officer, employee, or agent.

(d) An emergency exists for purposes of this section if a quorum of the corporation's directors cannot readily be assembled because of some catastrophic event. (1989, c. 265, s. 1.)

Article 3.

Purposes and Powers.

§ 55-3-01. Purposes.

(a) Every corporation incorporated under this Chapter has the purpose of engaging in any lawful business unless a more limited purpose is set forth in its articles of incorporation.

(b) A corporation engaging in a business that is subject to regulation under another statute of this State may incorporate under this Chapter only if permitted by, and subject to all limitations of, the other statute. (1955, c. 1371, s. 1; 1989, c. 265, s. 1.)

§ 55-3-02. General powers.

(a) Unless its articles of incorporation or this Chapter provide otherwise, every corporation has perpetual duration and succession in its corporate name and has the same powers as an individual to do all things necessary or convenient to carry out its business and affairs, including without limitation power:

(1) To sue and be sued, complain and defend in its corporate name;

(2) To have a corporate seal, which may be altered at will, and to use it, or a facsimile of it, by impressing or affixing it or in any other manner reproducing it;

(3) To make and amend bylaws, not inconsistent with its articles of incorporation or with the laws of this State, for managing the business and regulating the affairs of the corporation;

(4) To purchase, receive, lease, or otherwise acquire, and own, hold, improve, use, and otherwise deal with, real or personal property, or any legal or equitable interest in property, wherever located;

(5) To sell, convey, mortgage, pledge, lease, exchange, and otherwise dispose of all or any part of its property;

(6) To purchase, receive, subscribe for, or otherwise acquire; own, hold, vote, use, sell, mortgage, lend, pledge, or otherwise dispose of; and deal in and with shares or other interests in, or obligations of, any other entity;

(7) To make contracts and guarantees, incur liabilities, borrow money, issue its notes, bonds, and other obligations (which may be convertible into or include the option to purchase other securities of the corporation), and secure any of its obligations by mortgage or pledge of any of its property, franchises, or income;

(8) To lend money, invest and reinvest its funds, and receive and hold real and personal property as security for repayment;

(9) To be a promoter, partner, member, associate, or manager of any partnership, joint venture, trust, or other entity;

(10) To conduct its business, locate offices, and exercise the powers granted by this act within or without this State;

(11) To elect or appoint directors, officers, employees, and agents of the corporation, define their duties, fix their compensation, and lend them money and credit;

(12) To pay pensions and establish pension plans, pension trusts, profit sharing plans, stock bonus plans, stock option plans, and other benefit or incentive plans for any or all of its current or former directors, officers, employees, and agents;

(13) To make donations for the public welfare or for charitable, religious, cultural, scientific, or educational purposes;

(14) To transact any lawful business that will aid governmental policy;

(15) To make payments or donations, or do any other act, not inconsistent with law, that furthers the business and affairs of the corporation; and

(16) To provide insurance for its benefit on the life or physical or mental ability of any of its directors, officers or employees or on the life or physical or mental ability of any security holder for the purpose of acquiring at his death or disability its securities owned by such security holder, and for these purposes the corporation is deemed to have an insurable interest in its directors, officers, employees, or security holders; and to provide insurance for its benefit on the

life or physical or mental ability of any other person in whom it has an insurable interest.

(b) It shall not be necessary to set forth in the articles of incorporation any of the powers enumerated in this section. (Code, ss. 663, 666, 691, 692, 693; 1893, c. 159; 1901, c. 2, s. 1; Rev., s. 1128; 1909, c. 507, s. 1; C.S., s. 1126; 1925, cc. 235, 298; 1929, c. 269; 1939, c. 279; 1945, c. 775; G.S., s. 55-26; 1951, c. 1240, s. 1; 1955, c. 1371, s. 1; 1959, c. 1316, ss. 4, 5; 1969, c. 751, ss. 7, 8; 1989, c. 265, s. 1.)

§ 55-3-03. Emergency powers.

(a) In anticipation of or during an emergency defined in subsection (d), the board of directors of a corporation may:

(1) Modify lines of succession to accommodate the incapacity of any director, officer, employee, or agent; and

(2) Relocate the principal office, designate alternative principal offices or regional offices, or authorize the officers to do so.

(b) During an emergency defined in subsection (d), unless emergency bylaws provide otherwise:

(1) Notice of a meeting of the board of directors need be given only to those directors whom it is practicable to reach and may be given in any practicable manner, including by publication and radio; and

(2) One or more officers of the corporation present at a meeting of the board of directors may be deemed to be directors for the meeting, in order of rank and within the same rank in order of seniority, as necessary to achieve a quorum.

(c) Corporate action taken in good faith during an emergency under this section to further the ordinary business affairs of the corporation binds the corporation and the fact that said action is taken by special procedures may not be used to impose liability on a corporate director, officer, employee, or agent.

(d)   An emergency exists for purposes of this section if a quorum of the corporation's directors cannot readily be assembled because of some catastrophic event. (1989, c. 265, s. 1.)

§ 55-3-04. Ultra vires.

(a)   Except as provided in subsection (b), the validity of corporate action may not be challenged on the ground that the corporation lacks or lacked power to act.

(b)   A corporation's power to act may be challenged:

(1)   In a proceeding by a shareholder against the corporation to enjoin the act;

(2)   In a proceeding by the corporation, directly, derivatively, or through a receiver, trustee, or other legal representative, against an incumbent or former director, officer, employee, or agent of the corporation; or

(3)   In a proceeding by the Attorney General under G.S. 55-14-30.

(c)   In a shareholder's proceeding under subsection (b)(1) to enjoin an unauthorized corporate act, the court may enjoin or set aside the act, if equitable and if all affected persons are parties to the proceeding, and may award damages for loss (other than anticipated profits) suffered by the corporation or another party because of enjoining the unauthorized act. (Code, ss. 607, 686; 1901, c. 2, s. 107; Rev., s. 1197; C.S., s. 1143; G.S., 55-47; 1955, c. 1371, s. 1; 1989, c. 265, s. 1.)

§ 55-3-05. Exercise of corporate franchises not granted.

The Attorney General may upon his own information or upon complaint of a private party bring an action in the name of the State to restrain any person from exercising corporate franchises not granted. (Code, ss. 607, 686; 1901, c. 2, s. 107; Rev., s. 1197; C.S., s. 1143; G.S., s. 55-47(2); 1955, c. 1371, s. 1; 1989, c. 265, s. 1.)

Article 4.

Name.

§§ 55-4-01 through 55-4-05: Transferred to §§ 55D-20 through 55D-27 by Session Laws 2001-358, ss. 14(a) and 14(b).

Article 5.

Office and Agent.

§ 55-5-01. Registered office and registered agent.

Each corporation must maintain a registered office and registered agent as required by Article 4 of Chapter 55D of the General Statutes and is subject to service on the Secretary of State under that Article. (1901, c. 5; Rev., s. 1243; C.S., s. 1137; 1937, c. 133, ss. 1-3; G.S., ss. 55-38, 55-39; 1955, c. 1371, s. 1; 1957, c. 979, s. 17; 1989, c. 265, s. 1; 2000-140, s. 101(a); 2001-358, ss. 44, 47(a); 2001-387, ss. 173, 175(a); 2001-413, s. 6.)

§§ 55-5-02 through 55-5-04: Transferred to §§ 55D-31 through 55D-33 by Session Laws 2001-358, s. 44.

Article 6.

Shares and Distribution.

Part 1. Shares.

§ 55-6-01. Authorized shares.

(a)   The articles of incorporation must prescribe the classes of shares and the number of shares of each class that the corporation is authorized to issue. If more than one class of shares is authorized, the articles of incorporation must prescribe a distinguishing designation for each class, and, prior to the issuance of shares of a class, the preferences, limitations, and relative rights of that class must be described in the articles of incorporation. All shares of a class must have preferences, limitations, and relative rights identical with those of other shares of the same class unless the articles of incorporation divide a class into series. If a class is divided into series, all the shares of any one series must have preferences, limitations, and relative rights identical with those of other shares of the same series. The requirement of identical rights within a class shall not be construed to conflict with any special voting rights specified elsewhere in this Chapter.

(b)   Each series of a class must be given a distinguishing designation.

(c)   The articles of incorporation must authorize

(1)   One or more classes of shares that together have unlimited voting rights, and

(2)   One or more classes of shares (which may be the same class or classes as those with voting rights) that together are entitled to receive the net assets of the corporation upon dissolution.

(d)   The articles of incorporation may authorize one or more classes or series within a class of shares that:

(1)   Have special, conditional, or limited voting rights, or no right to vote, except to the extent prohibited by this Chapter;

(2)   Are redeemable or convertible as specified in the articles of incorporation (i) at the option of the corporation, the shareholder, or another person or upon the occurrence of a designated event; (ii) for cash, indebtedness, securities, or other property; (iii) in a designated amount or in an amount determined in accordance with a designated formula or by reference to extrinsic data or events;

(3) Entitle the holders to distributions calculated in any manner, including dividends that may be cumulative, noncumulative, or partially cumulative;

(4) Have preference over any other class or series within a class of shares with respect to distributions, including dividends and distributions upon the dissolution of the corporation.

(5) Notwithstanding the provisions of (d)(3) and (4) of this section, noncumulative preferred shares of a class or series within a class out of which shares were initially issued after June 30, 1957, and before October 1, 1969, shall be entitled to a dividend credit, as defined in this Chapter, and until such dividend credit is fully discharged no dividend shall be paid to any shares that are subordinate to such preferred shares as to dividends.

(e) The description of the designations, preferences, limitations, and relative rights in subsection (d) is not exhaustive. (1901, c. 2, s. 19; 1903, c. 660, ss. 2, 3; Rev., s. 1159; C.S., s. 1156; 1921, c. 116, s. 1; 1923, c. 155; C.S., s. 1167(a); 1925, c. 118, ss. 2, 2a; c. 262, s. 1; 1939, c. 199; 1949, c. 929; G.S., ss. 55-61, 55-73; 1953, c. 822, ss. 1, 3; 1955, c. 1371, s. 1; 1969, c. 751, ss. 15-17; 1985, c. 117, s. 1; 1989, c. 265, s. 1.)

§ 55-6-02. Terms of class or series determined by board of directors.

(a) If the articles of incorporation so provide, the board of directors may determine, in whole or part, the preferences, limitations, and relative rights (within the limits set forth in G.S. 55-6-01) of (1) any class of shares before the issuance of any shares of that class or (2) one or more series within a class before the issuance of any shares of that series.

(b) Before issuing any shares of a class or series created under this section, the corporation must deliver to the Secretary of State for filing articles of amendment, which are effective without shareholder action, that set forth:

(1) The name of the corporation;

(2) The text of the amendment determining the terms of the class or series of shares;

(3) The date it was adopted; and

(4)   A statement that the amendment was duly adopted by the board of directors. (1901, c. 2, s. 19; 1903, c. 660, ss. 2, 3; Rev., s. 1159; C.S., s. 1156; 1923, c. 155; 1925, c. 118, ss. 2, 2a; 1939, c. 199; G.S., s. 55-61; 1953, c. 822, s. 1; 1955, c. 1371, s. 1; 1989, c. 265, s. 1.)

§ 55-6-03. Issued and outstanding shares.

(a)   A corporation may issue the number of shares of each class or series authorized by the articles of incorporation. Shares that are issued are outstanding shares until they are reacquired, redeemed, converted, or cancelled.

(b)   The reacquisition, redemption, or conversion of outstanding shares is subject to the limitations of subsection (c) of this section and to G.S. 55-6-40.

(c)   At all times that shares of the corporation are outstanding, there must be outstanding one or more shares that together have unlimited voting rights and one or more shares that together are entitled to receive the net assets of the corporation upon dissolution. (1901, c. 2, s. 19; 1903, c. 660, ss. 2, 3; Rev., s. 1159; C.S., s. 1156; 1921, c. 116, s. 1; 1923, c. 155; C.S., s. 1167(a); 1925, c. 118, ss. 2, 2a; c. 262, s. 1; 1939, c. 199; 1949, c. 929; G.S., ss. 55-61, 55-73; 1953, c. 822, ss. 1, 3; 1955, c. 1371, s. 1; 1969, c. 751, ss. 15-17; 1985, c. 117, s. 1; 1989, c. 265, s. 1.)

§ 55-6-04. Fractional shares.

(a)   A corporation may:

(1)   Issue fractions of a share or pay in money the value of fractions of a share;

(2)   Arrange for disposition of fractional shares by the shareholders;

(3)   Issue scrip in registered or bearer form entitling the holder to receive a full share upon surrendering enough scrip to equal a full share.

(b) Each certificate representing scrip must be conspicuously labeled "scrip" and must contain the information required by G.S. 55-6-25(b).

(c) The holder of a fractional share is entitled to exercise the rights of a shareholder, including the right to vote, to receive dividends, and to participate in the assets of the corporation upon liquidation. The holder of scrip is not entitled to any of these rights unless the scrip provides for them.

(d) The board of directors may authorize the issuance of scrip subject to any condition considered desirable, including:

(1) That the scrip will become void if not exchanged for full shares before a specified date; and

(2) That the shares for which the scrip is exchangeable may be sold and the proceeds paid to the scripholders. (1955, c. 1371, s. 1; 1959, c. 1316, s. 20; 1989, c. 265, s. 1.)

§§ 55-6-05 through 55-6-19. Reserved for future codification purposes.

Part 2. Issuance of Shares.

§ 55-6-20. Subscription for shares before incorporation.

(a) A subscription for shares entered into before incorporation is irrevocable for six months unless the subscription agreement provides a longer or shorter period or all the subscribers agree to revocation.

(b) The board of directors may determine the payment terms of subscriptions for shares that were entered into before incorporation, unless the subscription agreement specifies them. A call for payment by the board of directors must be uniform so far as practicable as to all shares of the same class or series, unless the subscription agreement specifies otherwise.

(c) Shares issued pursuant to subscriptions entered into before incorporation are fully paid and nonassessable when the corporation receives the consideration specified in the subscription agreement.

(d) If a subscriber defaults in payment of money or property under a subscription agreement entered into before incorporation, the corporation may collect the amount owed as any other debt. Alternatively, unless the subscription agreement provides otherwise, the corporation may rescind the agreement and may sell the shares if the debt remains unpaid more than 20 days after the corporation sends written demand for payment to the subscriber.

(e) A subscription agreement entered into after incorporation is a contract between the subscriber and the corporation subject to G.S. 55-6-21. (1901, c. 2, ss. 23, 24, 25; Rev., ss. 1169, 1170, 1171; C.S., s. 1165; G.S., s. 55-70; 1955, c. 1371, s. 1; 1969, c. 751, s. 18; 1985, c. 117, s. 2; 1989, c. 265, s. 1.)

§ 55-6-21. Issuance of shares.

(a) The powers granted in this section to the board of directors may be reserved to the shareholders by the articles of incorporation. Unless the articles of incorporation or bylaws provide otherwise, the powers granted in this section to the board of directors may be delegated, within limits prescribed by the board of directors, to one or more officers of the corporation who are designated by the board of directors.

(b) The board of directors may authorize shares to be issued for consideration consisting of any tangible or intangible property or benefit to the corporation, including cash, promissory notes, services performed, contracts for services to be performed, or other securities of the corporation.

(c) Before the corporation issues shares, the board of directors must determine that the consideration received or to be received for shares to be issued is adequate. The determination by the board of directors as to the adequacy of consideration is conclusive as to whether the shares are validly issued, fully paid, and nonassessable.

(d) When the corporation receives the consideration for which the board of directors authorized the issuance of shares, the shares issued therefor are fully paid and nonassessable.

(e) The corporation may place in escrow shares issued for a contract for future services or benefits or for a promissory note, or make other arrangements to restrict the transfer of the shares, and may credit distributions in respect of the shares against their purchase price, until the services are performed, the note is paid, or the benefit received. If the services are not performed, the note is not paid, or the benefits are not received, the shares escrowed or restricted and the distributions credited may be cancelled in whole or part. (1901, c. 2, ss. 19, 53, 54; 1903, c. 660, ss. 2, 3; Rev. ss. 1159, 1160, 1161; C.S., ss. 1157, 1158; G.S., ss. 55-62, 55-63; 1955, c. 1371, s. 1; 1957, s. 1039; 1959, c. 1316, ss. 10, 13, 14; 1969, c. 751, s. 20; 1973, c. 469, ss. 15, 45.2; 1989, c. 265, s. 1; 1989 (Reg. Sess., 1990), c. 1024, s. 12.7; 2013-153, s. 1.)

§ 55-6-22. Liability of shareholders.

(a) A purchaser from a corporation of its own shares is not liable to the corporation or its creditors with respect to the shares except to pay the consideration for which the shares were authorized to be issued (G.S. 55-6-21) or specified in the subscription agreement (G.S. 55-6-20).

(b) Unless otherwise provided in the articles of incorporation, a shareholder of a corporation is not personally liable for the acts or debts of the corporation except that he may become personally liable by reason of his own acts or conduct. (1893, c. 471; 1901, c. 2, s. 22; Rev., s. 1162; C.S., s. 1160; G.S., s. 55-65; 1955, c. 1371, s. 1; 1969, c. 751, s. 28; 1989, c. 265. s. 1.)

§ 55-6-23. Share dividends.

(a) Unless the articles of incorporation provide otherwise, shares may be issued pro rata and without consideration to the corporation's shareholders or to the shareholders of one or more classes or series. An issuance of shares under this subsection is a share dividend.

(b) Shares of one class or series may not be issued as a share dividend in respect of shares of another class or series unless:

(1) The articles of incorporation so authorize,

(2) There are no outstanding shares of the class or series to be issued, or

(3)   A majority of the votes entitled to be cast by the class or series to be issued approve the issuance of not more than a stated number of shares within a period of not more than one year after such approval.

(c)   If the board of directors does not fix the record date for determining shareholders entitled to a share dividend, it is the date the board of directors authorizes the share dividend. (1955, c. 1371, s. 1; 1959, c. 1316, ss. 17, 18; 1989, c. 265, s. 1; 1989 (Reg. Sess., 1990), c. 1024, s. 12.8.)

§ 55-6-24. Rights, options, and warrants.

(a)   A corporation may issue rights, options, or warrants for the purchase of shares of the corporation. The board of directors, or officers of the corporation who are designated by the board of directors pursuant to G.S. 55-6-21(a), shall determine the terms upon which the rights, options, or warrants are issued, their form and content, and the consideration for which the shares are to be issued.

(b)   In the case of a public corporation, the terms and conditions of such rights, options or warrants may include, without limitation, restrictions or conditions that preclude or limit the exercise, transfer or receipt of such rights, options or warrants by the holder or holders or beneficial owner or owners of a specified number or percentage of the outstanding voting shares of such public corporation or by any transferee of any such holder or owner, or that invalidate or void such rights, options or warrants held by any such holder or owner or by such transferee. Determinations by the board of directors whether to impose, enforce, waive or otherwise render ineffective any such restrictions or conditions may be judicially reviewed in an appropriate proceeding. (1955, c. 1371, s. 1; 1959, c. 1316, s. 11; 1989, c. 265, s. 1; 2013-153, s. 2.)

§ 55-6-25. Form and content of certificates.

(a)   Shares may but need not be represented by certificates. Unless this act or another statute expressly provides otherwise, the rights and obligations of shareholders are identical whether or not their shares are represented by certificates.

(b)   At a minimum each share certificate must state on its face:

(1) The name of the issuing corporation and that it is organized under the law of North Carolina;

(2) The name of the person to whom issued; and

(3) The number and class of shares and the designation of the series, if any, the certificate represents.

(c) If the issuing corporation is authorized to issue different classes of shares or different series within a class, the designations, relative rights, preferences, and limitations applicable to each class and the variations in rights, preferences, and limitations determined for each series (and the authority of the board of directors to determine variations for future series) must be summarized on the front or back of each certificate. Alternatively, each certificate may state conspicuously on its front or back that the corporation will furnish the shareholder this information in writing and without charge.

(d) Each share certificate (1) must be signed (either manually or in facsimile) by two officers designated in the bylaws or by the board of directors and (2) may bear the corporate seal or its facsimile.

(e) If the person who signed in any capacity (either manually or in facsimile) a share certificate no longer holds office when the certificate is issued, the certificate is nevertheless valid. (1885, c. 265; 1901, c. 2, s. 94; Rev., ss. 1165, 1166; C.S., s. 1162; 1927, c. 173; 1949, c. 809; G.S., s. 55-67; 1955, c. 1371, s. 1; 1979, c. 91; 1989, c. 265, s. 1.)

§ 55-6-26. Shares without certificate.

(a) Unless the articles of incorporation or bylaws provide otherwise, the board of directors of a corporation may authorize the issue of some or all of the shares of any or all of its classes or series without certificates. The authorization does not affect shares already represented by certificates until they are surrendered to the corporation.

(b) Within a reasonable time after the issue or transfer of shares without certificates, the corporation shall send the shareholder a written statement of the information required on certificates by G.S. 55-6-25(b) and (c), and if applicable, G.S. 55-6-27. (1989, c. 265, s. 1.)

§ 55-6-27. Restriction on transfer of shares and other securities.

(a) The articles of incorporation, bylaws, an agreement among shareholders, or an agreement between shareholders and the corporation may impose restrictions on the transfer or registration of transfer of shares of the corporation. A restriction does not affect shares issued before the restriction was adopted unless the holders of the shares are parties to the restriction agreement or voted in favor of the restriction.

(b) A restriction on the transfer or registration of transfer of shares is valid and enforceable against the holder or a transferee of the holder if the restriction is authorized by this section, it is not unconscionable under the circumstances, and its existence is noted conspicuously on the front or back of the certificate or is contained in the information statement required by G.S. 55-6-26(b). Unless so noted, a restriction is not enforceable except against a person who receives actual written notice of the restrictions.

(c) A restriction on the transfer or registration of transfer of shares is authorized:

(1) To maintain the corporation's status when it is dependent on the number or identity of its shareholders;

(2) To preserve exemptions under federal or state securities law;

(3) For any other reasonable purpose.

(d) A restriction authorized by G.S. 55-6-27(c) may:

(1) Obligate the shareholder first to offer the corporation or other persons (separately, consecutively, or simultaneously) an opportunity to acquire the restricted shares;

(2) Obligate the corporation or other persons (separately, consecutively, or simultaneously) to acquire the restricted shares;

(3) Require the corporation, the holders of any class of its shares, or another person to approve the transfer of the restricted shares, if the requirement is not manifestly unreasonable;

(4) Prohibit the transfer of the restricted shares to designated persons or classes of persons, if the prohibition is not manifestly unreasonable;

(5) Contain any other provision reasonably related to an authorized purpose.

(e) For purposes of this section, "shares" includes a security convertible into or carrying a right to subscribe for or acquire shares. (1989, c. 265, s. 1.)

§ 55-6-28. Expense of issue.

A corporation may pay the expenses of selling or underwriting its shares, and of organizing or reorganizing the corporation, from the consideration received for shares. (1989, c. 265, s. 1.)

§ 55-6-29. Reserved for future codification purposes.

Part 3. Subsequent Acquisition of Shares by Shareholders and Corporation.

§ 55-6-30. Shareholders' preemptive rights.

(a) The shareholders of a corporation do not have a preemptive right to acquire the corporation's unissued shares except to the extent the articles of incorporation or subsection (d) of this section so provide.

(b) A statement included in the articles of incorporation that "the corporation elects to have preemptive rights" (or words of similar import) means that the following principles apply except to the extent the articles of incorporation expressly provide otherwise:

(1)   The shareholders of the corporation have a preemptive right, granted on uniform terms and conditions prescribed by the board of directors, to provide a fair and reasonable opportunity to exercise the right, to acquire proportional amounts of the corporation's unissued shares upon the decision of the board of directors to issue them.

(2)   A shareholder may waive his preemptive right. A waiver evidenced by a writing is irrevocable even though it is not supported by consideration.

(3)   There is no preemptive right with respect to (i) shares issued as compensation to directors, officers, agents, or employees of the corporation, its subsidiaries or affiliates; (ii) shares issued to satisfy conversion or option rights created to provide compensation to directors, officers, agents, or employees of the corporation, its subsidiaries or affiliates; (iii) shares authorized in articles of incorporation that are issued within six months from the effective date of incorporation; (iv) shares issued for considerations, other than money, deemed by the board of directors in good faith to be advantageous to the corporation's business.

(4)   Holders of a share of any class have no preemptive rights with respect to shares of any other class.

(5)   Reserved for future codification purposes.

(6)   Shares subject to preemptive rights that are not acquired by shareholders may be issued to any person during a period of one year after being offered to shareholders at a consideration set by the board of directors that is not lower than the consideration set for the exercise of preemptive rights. An offer at a lower consideration or after the expiration of one year is subject to the shareholders' preemptive rights.

(c)   For purposes of this section, "shares" includes a security convertible into or carrying a right to subscribe for or acquire shares.

(d)   Notwithstanding the foregoing provision of this section, shareholders of a corporation incorporated before July 1, 1990, other than a public corporation, shall have a preemptive right to acquire the unissued shares of the corporation, to the extent provided in (and subject to the limitations of) subdivisions (b) (1)-(6) and subsection (c) of this section, except to the extent the articles of incorporation expressly provide otherwise. (1955, c. 1371, s. 1; 1969, c. 751, ss. 29-32; 1979, c. 508, s. 2; 1989, c. 265, s. 1; 1993, c. 552, s. 8.)

§ 55-6-31. Corporation's acquisition of its own shares.

(a) A corporation may acquire its own shares and shares so acquired constitute authorized but unissued shares.

(b) If the articles of incorporation prohibit the reissue of the acquired shares, the number of authorized shares is reduced by the number of shares acquired, effective upon amendment of the articles of incorporation.

(c) Repealed by Session Laws 2005-268, s. 1, effective October 1, 2005. (1955, c. 1371, s. 1; 1957, c. 1039; 1959, c. 1316, s. 19; 1963, c. 666; 1967, c. 1163; 1969, c. 751, ss. 23-27, 45; 1973, c. 1067; 1985, c. 117, s. 3; 1989, c. 265, s. 1; 2005-268, s. 1.)

§§ 55-6-32 through 55-6-39. Reserved for future codification purposes.

Part 4. Distributions.

§ 55-6-40. Distributions to shareholders.

(a) A board of directors may authorize and the corporation may make distributions to its shareholders subject to restriction by the articles of incorporation and the limitation in subsection (c).

(b) If the board of directors does not fix the record date for determining shareholders entitled to a distribution (other than one involving a purchase, redemption, or other acquisition of the corporation's shares), it is the date the board of directors authorizes the distribution.

(c) No distribution may be made if, after giving it effect:

(1) The corporation would not be able to pay its debts as they become due in the usual course of business; or

(2) The corporation's total assets would be less than the sum of its total liabilities plus (unless the articles of incorporation permit otherwise) the amount that would be needed, if the corporation were to be dissolved at the time of the distribution, to satisfy the preferential rights upon dissolution of shareholders whose preferential rights are superior to those receiving the distribution.

(d) The board of directors may base a determination that a distribution is not prohibited under subsection (c) on financial statements prepared on the basis of accounting practices and principles that are reasonable in the circumstances, and may determine asset values either on book values or on a fair valuation or other method that is reasonable in the circumstances.

(e) Except as provided in subsection (g), the effect of a distribution under subsection (c) is measured:

(1) In the case of distribution by purchase, redemption, or other acquisition of the corporation's shares, as of the earlier of (i) the date money or other property is transferred or debt incurred by the corporation or (ii) the date the shareholder ceases to be a shareholder with respect to the acquired shares;

(2) In the case of any other distribution of indebtedness, as of the date the indebtedness is distributed;

(3) In all other cases, as of (i) the date the distribution is authorized if the payment occurs within 120 days after the date of authorization or (ii) the date the payment is made if it occurs more than 120 days after the date of authorization.

(f) A corporation's indebtedness to a shareholder incurred by reason of a distribution made in accordance with this section is at parity with the corporation's indebtedness to its general, unsecured creditors except to the extent otherwise provided by agreement.

(g) Indebtedness of a corporation, including indebtedness issued as a distribution, is not considered a liability for purposes of determinations under subsection (c) if its terms provide that payment of principal and interest are made only if and to the extent that payment of a distribution to shareholders could then be made under this section. If an indebtedness with such terms is issued as a distribution, each payment of principal or interest is treated as a distribution the effect of which is measured on the date the payment is actually made.

(h) Any action by a shareholder to compel the payment of dividends may be brought against the directors, or against the corporation with or without joining the directors as parties. The shareholder bringing such action shall be entitled, in the event that the court orders the payment of a dividend, to recover from the corporation all reasonable expenses, including attorney's fees, incurred in maintaining such action. If a court orders the payment of a dividend, the amount ordered to be paid shall be a debt of the corporation.

(i) As used in this subsection, net profits shall mean such net profits as can lawfully be paid in dividends to a particular class of shares after making allowance for the prior claims of shares, if any, entitled to preference in the payment of dividends. If during its immediately preceding fiscal period a corporation having less than 25 shareholders on the final day of said period has not paid to any class of shares dividends in cash or property amounting to at least one-third of the net profits of said period allocable to that class, the holder or holders of twenty percent (20%) or more of the shares of that class may, within four months after the close of said period, make written demand upon the corporation for the payment of additional dividends for that period. After a corporation has received such a demand, the directors shall, during the then current fiscal period or within three months after the close thereof, either (i) cause dividends in cash or property to be paid to the shareholders of that class in an amount equal to the difference between the dividends paid in said preceding fiscal period to shareholders of that class and one-third of the net profits of said period allocable to that class, or in such lesser amount as may be demanded, or (ii) give notice pursuant to subsection (j) of this section to all shareholders making such demand. Such corporation shall not, however, be required to pay dividends pursuant to such demand insofar as (i) such payment would exceed fifty percent (50%) of the net profits of the current fiscal period in which such demand is made, or (ii) the net profits are being retained to eliminate a deficit, or (iii) the payment of dividends would be a breach of a bona fide agreement between the corporation and its creditors restricting the payment of dividends, or (iv) the directors of the corporation can show that its earnings are being retained to meet the reasonably anticipated needs of the business and that such retention of earnings is not inequitable in light of all the circumstances. Upon receipt of such a demand a corporation may elect to treat any dividend previously paid in the current fiscal period as having been paid in the preceding fiscal period, in which event the corporation shall so notify all shareholders. If a dividend is paid in satisfaction of a demand made in accordance with this subsection it shall be deemed to have been paid in the period for which it was demanded, and all shareholders shall be so informed concurrently with such payment.

(j) Upon receipt of a demand from the holders of twenty percent (20%) or more of the shares of any class of shares pursuant to subsection (i) of this section, the corporation receiving such demand may, during the then fiscal period or within three months after the close thereof, give written notice to each shareholder making such written demand that the corporation elects to redeem all shares held by such shareholder in lieu of the payment of dividends as provided in subsection (i) of this section and shall pay to such shareholder the fair value of his shares as of the day preceding the mailing or otherwise reasonably dispatching of the notice. A shareholder receiving such notice shall thereafter be entitled to withdraw his dividend demand by giving written notice of such withdrawal to the corporation within 10 days after receipt of the redemption notice of the corporation or, if no such withdrawal is made, to receive the fair value of his shares, subject only to the surrender by him of the certificate or certificates representing his shares and to the provisions of G.S. 55-6-31, which value shall be determined and paid as follows:

(1) If within 30 days after the date upon which a shareholder becomes entitled to payment for his shares under this subsection, the value of the shares is agreed upon between the shareholder and the corporation, payment therefor shall be made within 60 days after the agreement, upon surrender of the certificate representing the shares, whereupon the shareholder shall cease to have any interest in such shares or in the corporation.

(2) If within the such 30-day period the shareholder and the corporation do not agree as to the value of the shares, the shareholder may, within 60 days after the expiration of the 30-day period, file a petition in the superior court of the county of the registered office of the corporation asking for the appointment by the clerk of three qualified and disinterested appraisers to appraise the fair value of the shares. A summons as in other cases of special proceedings, together with a copy of the petition, shall be served on the corporation at least 10 days prior to the hearing of the petition by the court. The award of appraisers, or a majority of them, if no exceptions be filed thereto within 10 days after the award shall have been filed in court, shall be confirmed by the court, and when confirmed shall be final and conclusive, and the shareholder upon depositing the proper share certificates in court, shall be entitled to judgment against the corporation for the appraised value thereof as of the date prescribed in this section, together with interest thereon to the date of such confirmation. If either party files exceptions to such award within 10 days after the award shall have

been filed in court, the case shall be transferred to the civil issue docket of the superior court for trial during term and shall be there tried in the same manner, as near as may be practicable, as is provided in Chapter 40A for the trial of cases under the eminent domain law of this State, and with the same right of appeal as is permitted in said Chapter. The court shall assess the cost of said proceedings as it shall deem equitable. Upon payment of the judgment the shareholder shall cease to have any interest in the shares or in the corporation and the corporation shall be entitled to have said share certificates surrendered to it by the clerk of court for cancellation. Unless the shareholder shall file such petition within the time herein prescribed, he and all persons claiming under him shall have no right of payment hereunder but in that event nothing herein shall impair his status as shareholder.

(k) Nothing in this section shall impair any rights which a shareholder may have on general principles of equity to compel the payment of dividends. (Code, s. 681; 1901, c. 2, ss. 33, 52; Rev., ss. 1191, 1192; C.S., ss. 1178, 1179; 1927, c. 121; 1933, c. 354, s. 1; G.S., ss. 55-115, 55-116; 1955, c. 1371, s. 1; 1957, c. 1039; 1959, c. 1316, ss. 16, 19, 35; 1963, c. 666; 1965, c. 726; 1967, c. 1163; 1969, c. 751, ss. 21-27, 45; 1973, c. 469, ss. 17-20, c. 683, c. 1067, c. 1087, ss. 3-5; 1975, c. 19, s. 17, c. 304; 1985, c. 117, s. 3; 1989, c. 265, s. 1; 1989 (Reg. Sess., 1990), c. 1024, s. 12.9; 1991, c. 645, s. 4.)

§ 55-7-09. Remote participation in meetings.

(a) To the extent authorized by a corporation's board of directors, shareholders of any class or series designated by the board of directors may participate in any meeting of shareholders by means of remote communication. Participation by means of remote communication shall be subject to such guidelines and procedures as the board of directors adopts and shall be in conformity with subsection (b) of this section.

(b) Shareholders participating in a shareholders' meeting by means of remote communication shall be deemed present and may vote at such a meeting if the corporation has implemented reasonable measures to do all of the following:

(1) Verify that each person participating remotely is a shareholder.

(2) Provide each shareholder participating remotely a reasonable opportunity to participate in the meeting and to vote on matters submitted to the shareholders, including an opportunity to communicate and read or hear the proceedings of the meeting, substantially concurrently with such proceedings. (2013-153, s. 5.)

Article 7.

Shareholders.

Part 1. Meetings.

§ 55-7-01. Annual meeting.

(a) A corporation shall hold a meeting of shareholders annually at a time stated in or fixed in accordance with the bylaws.

(b) Annual shareholders' meetings may be held in or out of this State at the place stated in or fixed in accordance with the bylaws. If no place is stated in or fixed in accordance with the bylaws, annual meetings shall be held at the corporation's principal office.

(c) The failure to hold an annual meeting at the time stated in or fixed in accordance with a corporation's bylaws does not affect the validity of any corporate action. Upon such failure, whether from lack of quorum or otherwise, a substitute annual meeting may be called in accordance with the provisions of G.S. 55-7-02 and any meeting so called may be designated as the annual meeting.

(d) Any matter relating to the affairs of a corporation that is appropriate for shareholder action is a proper subject for action at an annual meeting of shareholders, and unless required by some provision of this Chapter, the matter need not be specifically stated in the notice of meeting. (1901, c. 2, ss. 46, 49, 51; Rev., ss. 1179, 1188, 1190; C.S., ss. 1168, 1169, 1176; G.S., ss. 55-105, 55-106, 55-113; 1955, c. 1371, s. 1; 1959, c. 1316, ss. 21, 22; 1985 (Reg. Sess., 1986), c. 801, s. 44; 1989, c. 265. s. 1.)

§ 55-7-02. Special meeting.

(a)   A corporation shall hold a special meeting of shareholders:

(1)   On call of its board of directors or the person or persons authorized to do so by the articles of incorporation or the bylaws; or

(2)   In the case of a corporation that is not a public corporation, within 30 days after the holders of at least ten percent (10%) of all the votes entitled to be cast on any issue proposed to be considered at the proposed special meeting sign, date, and deliver to the corporation's secretary one or more written demands for the meeting describing the purpose or purposes for which it is to be held. The written demand shall cease to be effective on the sixty-first day after the date of signature appearing on the demand unless prior to the sixty-first day the corporation has received effective written demands from holders sufficient to call the special meeting.

(b)   If not otherwise fixed under G.S. 55-7-03 or G.S. 55-7-07, the record date for determining shareholders entitled to demand a special meeting is the date the first shareholder signs the demand.

(c)   Special shareholders' meetings may be held in or out of this State at the place stated in or fixed in accordance with the bylaws. If no place is stated or fixed in accordance with the bylaws, special meetings shall be held at the corporation's principal office.

(d)   Only business within the purpose or purposes described in the meeting notice required by G.S. 55-7-05(c) may be conducted at a special shareholders' meeting. (1901, c. 2, ss. 46, 49, 51; Rev., ss. 1179, 1188, 1190; C.S., ss. 1168, 1169, 1176; G.S., ss. 55-105, 55-106, 55-113; 1955, c. 1371, s. 1; 1959, c. 1316, ss. 21, 22; 1985 (Reg. Sess., 1986), c. 801, s. 44; 1989, c. 265, s. 1; 1991, c. 645, s. 17(a); 2001-201, s. 15; 2002-58, s. 1.)

§ 55-7-03. Court-ordered meeting.

(a) The superior court of the county where a corporation's principal office (or, if none in this State, its registered office) is located may, after notice is given to the corporation, summarily order a meeting to be held:

(1) On application of any shareholder if an annual meeting of the shareholders was not held within 15 months after the corporation's last annual meeting; or

(2) On application of a shareholder who signed a demand for a special meeting valid under G.S. 55-7-02, if the corporation does not proceed to hold the meeting as required by that section.

(b) The court may fix the time and place of the meeting, determine the shares entitled to participate in the meeting, specify a record date for determining shareholders entitled to notice of and to vote at the meeting, prescribe the form and content of the meeting notice, fix the quorum required for specific matters to be considered at the meeting (or direct that the votes represented at the meeting constitute a quorum for action on those matters), enter other orders necessary to accomplish the purpose or purposes of the meeting, and award such reasonable expenses, including attorneys' fees, as it deems appropriate. (1901, c. 2, ss. 46, 49, 51; Rev., ss. 1179, 1188, 1190; C.S., ss. 1168, 1169, 1176; G.S., ss. 55-105, 55-106, 55-113; 1955, c. 1371, s. 1; 1959, c. 1316, ss. 21, 22; 1985 (Reg. Sess., 1986), c. 801, s. 44; 1989, c. 265, s. 1; 1991, c. 645, s. 17(b).)

§ 55-7-04. Action without meeting.

(a) Action required or permitted by this Chapter to be taken at a shareholders' meeting may be taken without a meeting and without prior notice except as required by subsection (d) of this section, if the action is taken by all the shareholders entitled to vote on the action or, subject to subsection (a1) of this section, if so provided in the articles of incorporation of a corporation that is not a public corporation at the time the action is taken, by shareholders having not less than the minimum number of votes that would be necessary to take the action at a meeting at which all shareholders entitled to vote were present and voted. The action must be evidenced by one or more unrevoked written consents bearing the date of signature and signed by shareholders sufficient to take the action without a meeting, before or after such action, describing the action taken and delivered to the corporation for inclusion in the minutes or filing with the corporate records. To the extent the corporation has agreed pursuant to G.S. 55-1-50, a shareholder's consent to action taken without meeting or revocation thereof may be in electronic form and delivered by electronic means.

(a1) Notwithstanding subsection (a) of this section, the following actions may be taken without a meeting only by all the shareholders entitled to vote on the action:

(1) If cumulative voting is not authorized, the election of directors at the annual meeting; or

(2) If cumulative voting is authorized, the election of directors and the removal of a director unless the entire board of directors is to be removed, and if G.S. 55-7-28(e) applies to the corporation, an amendment to the articles of incorporation to deny or limit the right of shareholders to vote cumulatively and an amendment to the articles of incorporation or bylaws to decrease the number of directors.

(b) A shareholder's written consent to action to be taken without a meeting shall cease to be effective on the sixty-first day after the date of signature appearing on the consent unless prior to the sixty-first day the corporation has received unrevoked written consents sufficient under subsection (a) of this section to take the action without meeting. If not otherwise fixed under G.S. 55-7-03 or G.S. 55-7-07, the record date for determining shareholders entitled to take action without a meeting is the earliest date of signature appearing on any consent that is to be counted in satisfying the requirements of subsection (a) of this section. A shareholder may only revoke a written consent if such shareholder delivers to the corporation a written revocation prior to the corporation's receipt of unrevoked written consents sufficient under subsection (a) of this section to take the action.

(c) A consent signed under this section has the effect of a meeting vote and may be described as such in any document.

(d) Unless the articles of incorporation otherwise provide, if shareholder approval is required by this Chapter for (i) an amendment to the articles of incorporation pursuant to Article 10 of this Chapter, (ii) a plan of merger or share exchange pursuant to Article 11 of this Chapter, (iii) a plan of conversion pursuant to Part 2 of Article 11A of this Chapter, (iv) the sale, lease, exchange, or other disposition of all, or substantially all, of the corporation's property pursuant to Article 12 of this Chapter, or (v) a proposal for dissolution pursuant to Article 14 of this Chapter, and the approval is to be obtained through action without meeting, the corporation must give its shareholders, other than shareholders who consent to the action, written notice of the proposed action at least 10 days before the action is taken. The notice shall contain or be accompanied by the same material that, under this Chapter, would have been required to be sent to shareholders not entitled to vote on the action in a notice of meeting at which the proposed action would have been submitted to shareholders for action.

(e)   If action is taken without a meeting by fewer than all shareholders entitled to vote on the action, the corporation shall give written notice to all shareholders who have not consented to the action and who, if the action had been taken at a meeting, would have been entitled to notice of the meeting with the same record date as the action taken without a meeting, within 10 days after the action is taken. The notice shall describe the action and indicate that the action has been taken without a meeting of shareholders. Failure to comply with the requirements of this subsection shall not invalidate any action taken that otherwise complies with this section. (1955, c. 1371, s. 1; 1969, c. 751, s. 33; 1989, c. 265, s. 1; 2001-387, s. 11; 2001-487, ss. 62(b), 62(c); 2005-268, ss. 2, 3.)

§ 55-7-05. Notice of meeting.

(a)   A corporation shall notify shareholders of the date, time, and place of each annual and special shareholders' meeting no fewer than 10 nor more than 60 days before the meeting date. If the board of directors has authorized participation by means of remote communication pursuant to G.S. 55-7-09 for any class or series of shareholders, the notice to such class or series of shareholders shall describe the means of remote communication to be used. Unless this Chapter or the articles of incorporation require otherwise, the corporation is required to give notice only to shareholders entitled to vote at the meeting.

(b)   Unless this Chapter or the articles of incorporation require otherwise, notice of an annual meeting need not include a description of the purpose or purposes for which the meeting is called.

(c)   Notice of a special meeting must include a description of the purpose or purposes for which the meeting is called.

(d)   If not otherwise fixed under G.S. 55-7-03 or G.S. 55-7-07, the record date for determining shareholders entitled to notice of and to vote at an annual or special shareholders' meeting is the close of business on the day before the first notice is delivered to shareholders.

(e)   Unless the bylaws require otherwise, if an annual or special shareholders' meeting is adjourned to a different date, time, or place, notice need not be given of the new date, time, or place if the new date, time, or place is announced at the meeting before adjournment. If a new record date for the adjourned meeting is or must be fixed under G.S. 55-7-07, however, notice of the adjourned meeting must be given under this section to persons who are shareholders as of the new record date. (1955, c. 1371, s. 1; 1989, c. 265, s. 1; 2013-153, s. 3.)

§ 55-7-06. Waiver of notice.

(a)   A shareholder may waive any notice required by this Chapter, the articles of incorporation, or bylaws before or after the date and time stated in the notice. The waiver must be in writing, be signed by the shareholder entitled to the notice, and be delivered to the corporation for inclusion in the minutes or filing with the corporate records.

(b)   A shareholder's attendance at a meeting:

(1)   Waives objection to lack of notice or defective notice of the meeting, unless the shareholder at the beginning of the meeting objects to holding the meeting or transacting business at the meeting;

(2)   Waives objection to consideration of a particular matter at the meeting that is not within the purpose or purposes described in the meeting notice, unless the shareholder objects to considering the matter before it is voted upon. (1955, c. 1371, s. 1; 1989, c. 265, s. 1.)

§ 55-7-07. Record date.

(a) The bylaws may fix or provide the manner of fixing the record date for one or more voting groups in order to determine the shareholders entitled to notice of a shareholders' meeting, to demand a special meeting, to vote, or to take any other action. If the bylaws do not fix or provide for fixing a record date, the board of directors of the corporation may fix a future date as the record date.

(b) A record date fixed under this section may not be more than 70 days before the meeting or action requiring a determination of shareholders.

(c) A determination of shareholders entitled to notice of or to vote at a shareholders' meeting is effective for any adjournment of the meeting unless the board of directors fixes a new record date, which it must do if the meeting is adjourned to a date more than 120 days after the date fixed for the original meeting.

(d) If a court orders a meeting adjourned to a date more than 120 days after the date fixed for the original meeting, it may provide that the original record date continues in effect or it may fix a new record date. (1955, c. 1371, s. 1; 1973, c. 469, s. 45.1; 1989, c. 265, s. 1.)

§ 55-7-08: Repealed by Session Laws 2013-153, s. 4, effective January 1, 2014.

§ 55-7-10: Reserved for future codification purposes.

§ 55-7-11: Reserved for future codification purposes.

§ 55-7-12: Reserved for future codification purposes.

§ 55-7-13: Reserved for future codification purposes.

§ 55-7-14: Reserved for future codification purposes.

§ 55-7-15: Reserved for future codification purposes.

§ 55-7-16: Reserved for future codification purposes.

§ 55-7-17: Reserved for future codification purposes.

§ 55-7-18: Reserved for future codification purposes.

§ 55-7-19: Reserved for future codification purposes.

Part 2. Voting.

§ 55-7-20. Shareholders' list for meeting.

(a)   After fixing a record date for a meeting, a corporation shall prepare an alphabetical list of the names of all its shareholders who are entitled to notice of a shareholders' meeting. The list must be arranged by voting group (and within each voting group by class or series of shares) and show the address of and number of shares held by each shareholder.

(b)   The shareholders' list must be available for inspection by any shareholder, beginning two business days after notice of the meeting is given for which the list was prepared and continuing through the meeting, at the corporation's principal office or at a place identified in the meeting notice in the city where the meeting will be held. A shareholder, personally or by or with his representative, is entitled on written demand to inspect and, subject to the requirements of G.S. 55-16-02(c), to copy the list, during regular business hours and at his expense, during the period it is available for inspection.

(c) The corporation shall make the shareholders' list available at the meeting, and any shareholder, personally or by or with his representative, is entitled to inspect the list at any time during the meeting or any adjournment. The corporation is not required to make the list available through electronic or other means of remote communication to a shareholder or proxy attending the meeting by remote communication pursuant to G.S. 55-7-09.

(d) If the corporation refuses to allow a shareholder or his representative to inspect the shareholders' list before or at the meeting (or copy the list as permitted by subsection (b)), the superior court of the county where a corporation's principal office (or, if none in this State, its registered office) is located, on application of the shareholder, after notice is given to the corporation, may summarily order the inspection or copying at the corporation's expense and may postpone the meeting for which the list was prepared until the inspection or copying is complete.

(e) Refusal or failure to prepare or make available the shareholders' list does not affect the validity of action taken at the meeting. (1955, c. 1371, s. 1; 1989, c. 265, s. 1; 1993, c. 552, s. 9; 2001-387, s. 13; 2013-153, s. 6.)

§ 55-7-21. Voting entitlement of shares.

(a) Except as provided in subsections (b) and (c) or unless the articles of incorporation provide otherwise, each outstanding share, regardless of class, is entitled to one vote on each matter voted on at a shareholders' meeting.

(b) Absent special circumstances, the shares of a corporation are not entitled to vote if they are owned, directly or indirectly, by a second corporation, domestic or foreign, and the first corporation owns, directly or indirectly, a majority of the shares entitled to vote for directors of the second corporation.

(c) Subsection (b) does not limit the power of a corporation to vote any shares, including its own shares, held by it in a fiduciary capacity.

(d) Redeemable shares are not entitled to vote after notice of redemption is given to the holders and a sum sufficient to redeem the shares has been deposited with a bank, trust company, or other financial institution under an irrevocable obligation to pay the holders the redemption price on surrender of the shares. (Rev., ss. 1183, 1184; 1907, c. 457, s. 1; 1909, c. 827, s. 1; C.S., s. 1173; 1945, c. 635; G.S., s. 55-110; 1951, c. 265, s. 2; 1953, c. 722; 1955, c. 1371, s. 1; 1959, c. 768; c. 1316, s. 23; 1963, c. 1065; 1969, c. 751, ss. 34, 35; 1985, c. 419; 1985 (Reg. Sess., 1986), c. 801, s. 45; 1989, c. 265, s. 1.)

§ 55-7-21.1. Rights of holders of debt securities.

In addition to any rights otherwise lawfully conferred, the articles of incorporation of the corporation may confer upon the holders of any bonds, debentures or other debt obligations issued or to be issued by the corporation any one or more of the following powers and rights upon such terms and conditions as may be prescribed in the articles of incorporation:

(1) The power to vote on any matter either in conjunction with or to the full or partial exclusion of its shareholders, notwithstanding G.S. 55-6-01(c)(1), and in determination of votes and voting groups, the holders of such debt obligations shall be treated as shareholders;

(2) The right to inspect the corporate books and records;

(3) Any other rights concerning the corporation which its shareholders have or may have.

Any such power or right shall not be diminished, as to bonds, debentures or other obligations then outstanding, except by an amendment of the articles of incorporation approved by the vote or written consent of the holders of a majority in principal amount thereof or such larger percentage as may be specified in the articles of incorporation. (1969, c. 751, s. 19; 1989, c. 265, s. 1; 1989 (Reg. Sess., 1990), c. 1024, s. 12.10; 1991, c. 645, s. 5.)

§ 55-7-22. Proxies.

(a) A shareholder may vote his shares in person or by proxy.

(b) A shareholder may appoint one or more proxies to vote or otherwise act for the shareholder by signing an appointment form, either personally or by the shareholder's attorney-in-fact. Without limiting G.S. 55-1-50, an appointment in the form of an electronic record that bears the shareholder's electronic signature and that may be directly reproduced in paper form by an automated process shall be deemed a valid appointment form within the meaning of this section. In addition, a public corporation may permit a shareholder may to appoint one or more proxies by any kind of telephonic transmission, even if not accompanied by written communication, under circumstances or together with information from which the corporation can reasonably assume that the appointment was made or authorized by the shareholder.

(c) An appointment of a proxy is effective when received by the secretary or other officer or agent authorized to tabulate votes. An appointment is valid for 11 months unless a different period is expressly provided in the appointment form.

(d) An appointment of a proxy is revocable by the shareholder unless the appointment form conspicuously states that it is irrevocable and the appointment is coupled with an interest. Appointments coupled with an interest include the appointment of:

(1) A pledgee;

(2) A person who purchased or agreed to purchase the shares;

(3) A creditor of the corporation who extended it credit under terms requiring the appointment;

(4) An employee of the corporation whose employment contract requires the appointment; or

(5) A party to a voting agreement created under G.S. 55-7-31.

(e) The death or incapacity of the shareholder appointing a proxy does not affect the right of the corporation to accept the proxy's authority unless notice of the death or incapacity is received by the secretary or other officer or agent authorized to tabulate votes before the proxy exercises his authority under the appointment.

(f) An appointment made irrevocable under subsection (d) shall be revocable when the interest with which it is coupled is extinguished.

(g) A transferee for value of shares subject to an irrevocable appointment may revoke the appointment if he did not know of its existence when he acquired the shares and the existence of the irrevocable appointment was not noted conspicuously on the certificate representing the shares or on the information statement for shares without certificates.

(h) Subject to G.S. 55-7-24 and to any express limitation on the proxy's authority appearing on the face of the appointment form, a corporation is entitled to accept the proxy's vote or other action as that of the shareholder making the appointment. (1955, c. 1371, s. 1; 1959, c. 1316, s. 24; 1973, c. 469, ss. 23-25; 1989, c. 265, s. 1; 1999-138, s. 1; 2001-387, s. 14.)

§ 55-7-23. Shares held by nominees.

(a) A corporation may establish a procedure by which the beneficial owner of shares that are registered in the name of a nominee is recognized by the corporation as a shareholder. The extent of this recognition may be determined in the procedure.

(b) The procedure may set forth:

(1) The types of nominees to which it applies;

(2) The rights or privileges that the corporation recognizes in a beneficial owner;

(3) The manner in which the procedure is selected by the nominee;

(4) The information that must be provided when the procedure is selected;

(5) The period for which selection of the procedure is effective; and

(6) Other aspects of the rights and duties created. (1989, c. 265, s. 1.)

§ 55-7-24. Corporation's acceptance of votes.

(a)   If the name signed on a vote, consent, waiver, or proxy appointment corresponds to the name of a shareholder, the corporation if acting in good faith is entitled to accept the vote, consent, waiver, or proxy appointment and give it effect as the act of the shareholder.

(b)   If the name signed on a vote, consent, waiver, or proxy appointment does not correspond to the name of its shareholder, the corporation if acting in good faith is nevertheless entitled to accept the vote, consent, waiver, or proxy appointment and give it effect as the act of the shareholder if:

(1)   The shareholder is an entity and the name signed purports to be that of an officer or agent of the entity;

(2)   The name signed purports to be that of an administrator, executor, guardian, or conservator representing the shareholder and, if the corporation requests, evidence of fiduciary status acceptable to the corporation has been presented with respect to the vote, consent, waiver, or proxy appointment;

(3)   The name signed purports to be that of a receiver or trustee in bankruptcy of the shareholder and, if the corporation requests, evidence of its status acceptable to the corporation has been presented with respect to the vote, consent, waiver, or proxy appointment;

(4)   The name signed purports to be that of a pledgee, beneficial owner, or attorney-in-fact of the shareholder and, if the corporation requests, evidence acceptable to the corporation of the signatory's authority to sign for the shareholder has been presented with respect to the vote, consent, waiver, or proxy appointment;

(5)   Two or more persons are the shareholder as co-tenants or fiduciaries and the name signed purports to be the name of at least one of the co-owners and the person signing appears to be acting on behalf of all the co-owners.

(c)   The corporation is entitled to reject a vote, consent, waiver, or proxy appointment if the secretary or other officer or agent authorized to tabulate votes, acting in good faith, has reasonable basis for doubt about the validity of the signature on it or about the signatory's authority to sign for the shareholder.

(d) The corporation and its officer or agent who accepts or rejects a vote, consent, waiver, or proxy appointment in good faith and in accordance with the standards of this section or G.S. 55-7-22(b) are not liable in damages to the shareholder for the consequences of the acceptance or rejection.

(e) Corporate action based on the acceptance or rejection of a vote, consent, waiver, or proxy appointment under this section is valid unless a court of competent jurisdiction determines otherwise. (1901, c. 2, ss. 42, 43; c. 474, ss. 1, 2; Rev., ss. 1185, 1186, 1187; C.S., s. 1174; G.S., s. 55-111; 1955, c. 1371, s. 1; 1957, c. 1039; 1959, c. 1316, s. 36; 1989, c. 265, s. 1; 2005-268, ss. 4, 5.)

§ 55-7-25. Quorum and voting requirements for voting groups.

(a) Shares entitled to vote as a separate voting group may take action on a matter at a meeting only if a quorum of that voting group exists with respect to that matter, except that, in the absence of a quorum at the opening of any meeting of shareholders, such meeting may be adjourned from time to time by the vote of a majority of the votes cast on the motion to adjourn. Unless the articles of incorporation, a bylaw adopted by the shareholders, or this act provides otherwise, a majority of the votes entitled to be cast on the matter by the voting group constitutes a quorum of that voting group for action on that matter.

(b) Once a share is represented for any purpose at a meeting, it is deemed present for quorum purposes for the remainder of the meeting and for any adjournment of that meeting unless a new record date is or must be set for that adjourned meeting.

(c) If a quorum exists, action on a matter (other than the election of directors) by a voting group is approved if the votes cast within the voting group favoring the action exceed the votes cast opposing the action, unless the articles of incorporation, a bylaw adopted by the shareholders, or this Chapter requires a greater number of affirmative votes.

(d) An amendment of the articles of incorporation or bylaws adding, changing, or deleting a quorum or voting requirement for a voting group greater than specified in subsection (a) or (c) is governed by G.S. 55-7-27.

(e) The election of directors is governed by G.S. 55-7-28. (1901, c. 2, s. 39; Rev., s. 1182; C.S., s. 1175; 1927, c. 138; G.S., s. 55-112; 1955, c. 1371, s. 1; 1973, c. 469, ss. 21, 22; 1989, c. 265, s. 1; 1991, c. 645, s. 16(a).)

§ 55-7-26. Action by single and multiple voting groups.

(a) If the articles of incorporation, a bylaw adopted by the shareholders, or this Chapter provides for voting by a single voting group on a matter, action on that matter is taken when voted upon by that voting group as provided in G.S. 55-7-25.

(b) If the articles of incorporation, a bylaw adopted by the shareholders, or this Chapter provides for voting by two or more voting groups on a matter, action on that matter is taken only when voted upon by each of those voting groups counted separately as provided in G.S. 55-7-25. Action may be taken by one voting group on a matter even though no action is taken at the same time by another voting group entitled to vote on the matter. (1989, c. 265, s. 1.)

§ 55-7-27. Greater quorum or voting requirements.

(a) The articles of incorporation or a bylaw adopted by the shareholders may provide for a greater quorum or voting requirement for shareholders (or voting groups of shareholders) than is provided for by this Chapter. Any such bylaw adopted by the shareholders after the effective date of this section must be approved by a quorum and vote sufficient to amend the articles of incorporation for that purpose.

(b) Any provision in the articles of incorporation or bylaws prescribing the quorum or vote required for any purpose as permitted by this section may not itself be amended by a quorum or vote less than the quorum or vote therein prescribed. (1955, c. 1371, s. 1; 1959, c. 1316, ss. 2, 3; 1973, c. 469, ss. 4, 22; 1989, c. 265, s. 1.)

§ 55-7-28. Voting for directors; cumulative voting.

(a) Unless otherwise provided in the articles of incorporation or in an agreement valid under G.S. 55-7-31, directors are elected by a plurality of the votes cast by the shares entitled to vote in the election at a meeting at which a quorum is present.

(b) Except as provided in subsection (e) of this section, shareholders do not have a right to cumulate their votes for directors unless the articles of incorporation so provide.

(c) A statement included in the articles of incorporation that "[all] [a designated voting group of] shareholders are entitled to cumulate their votes for directors" (or words of similar import) means that the shareholders designated are entitled to multiply the number of votes they are entitled to cast by the number of directors for whom they are entitled to vote and cast the product for a single candidate or distribute the product among two or more candidates.

(d) Shares otherwise entitled to vote cumulatively may not be voted cumulatively at a particular meeting unless:

(1) The meeting notice or proxy statement accompanying the notice states conspicuously that cumulative voting is authorized; or

(2) A shareholder or proxy who has the right to cumulate his votes announces in open meeting, before voting for directors starts, his intention to vote cumulatively; and if such announcement is made, the chair shall declare that all shares entitled to vote have the right to vote cumulatively and shall announce the number of votes represented in person and by proxy, and shall thereupon grant a recess of not less than one hour nor more than four hours, as he shall determine, or of such other period of time as is unanimously then agreed upon.

(e) Shareholders of a corporation incorporated in this State shall have the right to cumulate their votes for directors if

(1) The corporation was in existence prior to July 1, 1957, under a charter which does not grant the right of cumulative voting and at the time of the election the stock transfer book of such corporation discloses, or it otherwise appears, that there is at least one stockholder who owns or controls more than one-fourth of the voting stock of such corporation (shares represented at a meeting by revocable proxy relating to that meeting or adjourned meetings

thereof shall not be deemed shares "controlled" within the meaning of this subsection), or if

(2)   The corporation was incorporated on or after July 1, 1957, and before July 1, 1990,

unless, when the stock transfer books are closed or at the record date fixed to determine the shareholders entitled to receive notice of and to vote at the meeting of shareholders, the corporation is a public corporation as defined in G.S. 55-1-40(18a). This right to vote cumulatively may be denied or limited by amendment to the articles of incorporation, but no such amendment shall be made when the number of shares voting against the amendment would be sufficient to elect a director by cumulative voting if such shares are entitled to be voted cumulatively for the election of directors. (Rev., ss. 1183, 1184; 1907, c. 457, s. 1; 1909, c. 827, s. 1; C.S., s. 1173; 1945, c. 635; G.S., s. 55-110; 1951, c. 265, s. 2; 1953, c. 722; 1955, c. 1371, s. 1; 1959, c. 768; c. 1316, s. 23; 1963, c. 1065; 1969, c. 751, ss. 34, 35; 1985, c. 419; 1985 (Reg. Sess., 1986), c. 801, s. 45; 1989, c. 265, s. 1; 1989 (Reg. Sess., 1990), c. 1024, s. 12.11; 1991, c. 645, ss. 16(b), 19.)

§ 55-7-29. Reserved for future codification purposes.

Part 3. Voting Trusts and Agreements.

§ 55-7-30. Voting trusts.

(a)   One or more shareholders may create a voting trust, conferring on a trustee the right to vote or otherwise act for them, by signing an agreement setting out the provisions of the trust (which may include anything consistent with its purpose) and transferring their shares to the trustee. When a voting trust agreement is signed, the trustee shall prepare a list of the names and addresses of all owners of beneficial interests in the trust, together with the number and class of shares each transferred to the trust, and deliver copies of the list and agreement to the corporation's principal office.

(b) A voting trust becomes effective on the date the first shares subject to the trust are registered in the trustee's name. A voting trust is valid for not more than 10 years after its effective date unless extended under subsection (c).

(c) All or some of the parties to a voting trust may extend it for additional terms of not more than 10 years each by signing an extension agreement and obtaining the voting trustee's written consent to the extension. An extension is valid for not more than 10 years from the date the first shareholder signs the extension agreement. The voting trustee must deliver copies of the extension agreement and list of beneficial owners to the corporation's principal office. An extension agreement binds only those parties signing it. (1955, c. 1371, s. 1; 1963, c. 1233; 1973, c. 469, ss. 26-28; 1989, c. 265, s. 1.)

§ 55-7-31. Shareholders' agreements.

(a) An agreement between two or more shareholders, if in writing and signed by the parties thereto, may provide that in the exercise of any voting rights of shares held by the parties, including any vote with respect to directors, such shares shall be voted as provided by the agreement, or as the parties may agree, or as determined in accordance with any procedure (including arbitration) specified in the agreement. Such agreement shall be valid as between the parties thereto for not more than 10 years from the date of its execution. A voting agreement created under this section may be extended or renewed in like manner as a voting trust may be extended or renewed as provided by G.S. 55-7-30 (c), but is not otherwise subject to the provisions of G.S. 55-7-30.

(b) Except in the case of a public corporation, no written agreement to which all of the shareholders have actually assented, whether embodied in the articles of incorporation or bylaws or in any side agreement in writing and signed by all the parties thereto, and which relates to any phase of the affairs of the corporation, whether to the management of its business or division of its profits or otherwise, shall be invalid as between the parties thereto, on the ground that it is an attempt by the parties thereto to treat the corporation as if it were a partnership or to arrange their relationships in a manner that would be appropriate between partners. A transferee of shares covered by such agreement who acquires them with knowledge thereof is bound by its provisions.

(c) A written agreement between all or less than all of the shareholders, whether solely between themselves or between one or more of them and a party who is not a shareholder, is not invalid as between the parties thereto on the ground that it so relates to the conduct of the affairs of the corporation as to interfere with the discretion of the board of directors. The effect of any such agreement shall be to relieve the directors and impose upon the shareholders who are parties to the agreement the liability for managerial acts or omissions which is imposed on directors to the extent and so long as the discretion or powers of the board in its management of corporate affairs is controlled by such agreement. (1955, c. 1371, s. 1; 1973, c. 469, s. 29; 1981 (Reg. Sess., 1982), c. 1163; 1989, c. 265, s. 1.)

§§ 55-7-32 through 55-7-39. Reserved for future codification purposes.

Part 4. Derivative Proceedings.

§ 55-7-40. Shareholders' derivative actions.

Subject to the provisions of G.S. 55-7-41 and G.S. 55-7-42, a shareholder may bring a derivative proceeding in the superior court of this State. The superior court has exclusive original jurisdiction over shareholder derivative actions. (1973, c. 469, s. 12; 1989, c. 265, s. 1; 1995, c. 149, s. 1.)

§ 55-7-40.1. Definitions.

In this Part:

(1) "Derivative proceeding" means a civil suit in the right of a domestic corporation or, to the extent provided in G.S. 55-7-47, in the right of a foreign corporation.

(2) "Shareholder" has the same meaning as in G.S. 55-1-40 and includes a beneficial owner whose shares are held in a voting trust or held by a nominee on the beneficial owner's behalf. (1995, c. 149, s. 1.)

§ 55-7-41. Standing.

A shareholder may not commence or maintain a derivative proceeding unless the shareholder:

(1)   Was a shareholder of the corporation at the time of the act or omission complained of or became a shareholder through transfer by operation of law from one who was a shareholder at that time; and

(2)   Fairly and adequately represents the interests of the corporation in enforcing the right of the corporation. (1995, c. 149, s. 1.)

§ 55-7-42. Demand.

No shareholder may commence a derivative proceeding until:

(1)   A written demand has been made upon the corporation to take suitable action; and

(2)   90 days have expired from the date the demand was made unless, prior to the expiration of the 90 days, the shareholder was notified that the corporation rejected the demand, or unless irreparable injury to the corporation would result by waiting for the expiration of the 90-day period. (1995, c. 149, s. 1.)

§ 55-7-43. Stay of proceedings.

If the corporation commences an inquiry into the allegations set forth in the demand or complaint, the court may stay a derivative proceeding for a period of time the court deems appropriate. (1995, c. 149, s. 1.)

§ 55-7-44. Dismissal.

(a) The court shall dismiss a derivative proceeding on motion of the corporation if one of the groups specified in subsection (b) or (f) of this section determines in good faith after conducting a reasonable inquiry upon which its conclusions are based that the maintenance of the derivative proceeding is not in the best interest of the corporation.

(b) Unless a panel is appointed pursuant to subsection (f) of this section, the inquiry and determination shall be made by:

(1) A majority vote of independent directors present at a meeting of the board of directors if the independent directors constitute a quorum; or

(2) A majority vote of a committee consisting of two or more independent directors appointed by majority vote of independent directors present at a meeting of the board of directors, whether or not the independent directors constituted a quorum.

(c) For purposes of this section, none of the following factors by itself shall cause a director to be considered not independent:

(1) The nomination or election of the director by persons who are defendants in the derivative proceeding or against whom action is demanded;

(2) The naming of the director as a defendant in the derivative proceeding or as a person against whom action is demanded; or

(3) The approval by the director of the act being challenged in the derivative proceeding or demand if the act resulted in no personal benefit to the director.

(d) If a derivative proceeding is commenced after a determination has been made rejecting a demand by a shareholder, the complaint shall allege with particularity facts establishing that the requirements of subsection (a) of this section have not been met. Defendants may make a motion to dismiss a complaint under subsection (a) of this section for failure to comply with this subsection. Prior to the court's ruling on such a motion to dismiss, the plaintiff shall be entitled to discovery only with respect to the issues presented by the motion and only if and to the extent that the plaintiff has alleged such facts with particularity. The preliminary discovery shall be limited solely to matters germane and necessary to support the facts alleged with particularity relating solely to the requirements of subsection (a) of this section.

(e) If a majority of the board of directors does not consist of independent directors at the time the determination is made, the corporation shall have the burden of proving that the requirements of subsection (a) of this section have been met. If a majority of the board of directors consists of independent directors at the time the determination is made, the plaintiff shall have the burden of proving that the requirements of subsection (a) of this section have not been met.

(f) The court may appoint a panel of one or more independent persons upon motion of the corporation to make a determination whether the maintenance of the derivative proceeding is in the best interest of the corporation. The plaintiff shall have the burden of proving that the requirements of subsection (a) of this section have not been met. (1995, c. 149, s. 1; c. 509, s. 135.2(t).)

§ 55-7-45. Discontinuance or settlement.

(a) A derivative proceeding may not be discontinued or settled without the court's approval. If the court determines that a proposed discontinuance or settlement will substantially affect the interests of the corporation's shareholders or a class of shareholders, the court shall direct that notice be given to the shareholders affected.

(b) The court shall determine the manner and form of the notice and the manner in which costs of the notice shall be borne. (1995, c. 149, s. 1.)

§ 55-7-46. Payment of expenses.

On termination of the derivative proceeding, the court may:

(1) Order the corporation to pay the plaintiff's reasonable expenses, including attorneys' fees, incurred in the proceeding if it finds that the proceeding has resulted in a substantial benefit to the corporation;

(2) Order the plaintiff to pay any defendant's reasonable expenses, including attorneys' fees, incurred in defending the proceeding if it finds that the

proceeding was commenced or maintained without reasonable cause or for an improper purpose; or

(3) Order a party to pay an opposing party's reasonable expenses, including attorneys' fees, incurred as a result of the filing of a pleading, motion, or other paper, if the court, after reasonable inquiry, finds that the pleading, motion, or other paper was not well grounded in fact or was not warranted by existing law or a good faith argument for the extension, modification, or reversal of existing law, and that it was interposed for an improper purpose, such as to harass or to cause unnecessary delay or needless increase in the cost of litigation. (1995, c. 149, s. 1.)

§ 55-7-47. Applicability to foreign corporations.

In any derivative proceeding in the right of a foreign corporation, the matters covered by this Part shall be governed by the laws of the jurisdiction of incorporation of the foreign corporation except for the matters governed by G.S. 55-7-43, 55-7-45, and 55-7-46. (1995, c. 149, s. 1.)

§ 55-7-48. Suits against directors of public corporations.

In addition to the requirements of this Part, the plaintiff in an action brought on behalf of a corporation that is a public corporation at the time of the action against one or more of its directors for monetary damages shall:

(1) Allege, and it must appear, that each plaintiff has been a shareholder or holder of a beneficial interest in shares of the corporation for at least one year;

(2) Bring the action within two years of the date of the transaction of which the plaintiff complains; and

(3) If the court orders, execute and deposit with the clerk of court a written undertaking with sufficient surety, approved by the court, to indemnify the corporation against any and all expenses reasonably expected to be incurred by the corporation in connection with the proceeding, including expenses arising by way of indemnity. (1995, c. 149, s. 1.)

§ 55-7-49. Privileged communications.

In any derivative proceeding, no shareholder shall be entitled to obtain or have access to any communication within the scope of the corporation's attorney-client privilege that could not be obtained by or would not be accessible to a party in an action other than on behalf of the corporation. (1995, c. 149, s. 1.)

Article 8.

Directors and Officers.

Part 1. Board of Directors.

§ 55-8-01. Requirement for and duties of board of directors.

(a) Except as provided in subsection (c), each corporation must have a board of directors.

(b) All corporate powers shall be exercised by or under the authority of, and the business and affairs of the corporation managed by or under the direction of, its board of directors, except as otherwise provided in the articles of incorporation or in an agreement valid under G.S. 55-7-31(b).

(c) A corporation may dispense with or limit the authority of a board of directors by describing in its articles of incorporation or in an agreement valid under G.S. 55-7-31(b) who will perform some or all of the duties of a board of directors; but no such limitation upon the authority which the board of directors would otherwise have shall be effective against other persons without actual knowledge of such limitation.

(d) To the extent the articles of incorporation or an agreement valid under G.S. 55-7-31(b) vests authority of the board of directors in an individual or group other than the board of directors, such individual or group in the exercise of such authority shall be deemed to be acting as the board of directors for all purposes of this Chapter. (1955, c. 1371, s. 1; 1989, c. 265, s. 1; 2005-268, s. 6.)

§ 55-8-02. Qualifications of directors.

The articles of incorporation or bylaws may prescribe qualifications for directors. A director need not be a resident of this State or a shareholder of the corporation unless the articles of incorporation or bylaws so prescribe. (1955, c. 1371, s. 1; 1989, c. 265, s. 1.)

§ 55-8-03. Number and election of directors.

(a) A board of directors must consist of one or more individuals, with the number specified in or fixed in accordance with the articles of incorporation or bylaws.

(b) The number of directors may be increased or decreased from time to time by amendment to, or in the manner provided in, the articles of incorporation or the bylaws, but for a corporation to which G.S. 55-7-28(e) applies in which shares are entitled to be voted cumulatively, the number of directors shall not be decreased unless one of the following applies:

(1) The decrease is approved by the shareholders in a vote in which the number of shares entitled to be voted cumulatively that vote against the proposal for decrease would not be sufficient to elect a director by cumulative voting.

(2) The decrease is made pursuant to a provision of the articles of incorporation or bylaws fixing a minimum and maximum number of directors and authorizing the number of directors to be fixed or changed from time to time, within the maximum and the minimum, by the shareholders or, unless the articles of incorporation or an agreement valid under G.S. 55-7-31 provides otherwise, the board of directors.

(c) Repealed by Session Laws 2005-268, s. 7.

(d) Directors are elected at the first annual shareholders' meeting and at each annual meeting thereafter unless their terms are staggered under G.S. 55-8-06. (1901, c. 2, ss. 14, 39; Rev., ss. 1147, 1182; C.S., ss. 1144, 1175; 1927, c. 138; G.S., ss. 55-48, 55-112; 1955, c. 1371, s. 1; 1959, c. 1316, s. 33; 1969, c. 751, ss. 10, 11; 1989, c. 265, s. 1; 1993, c. 552, s. 13; 2005-268, s. 7; 2006-264, s. 44(a).)

§ 55-8-04. Election of directors by certain classes of shareholders.

If the articles of incorporation authorize dividing the shares into classes, the articles may also authorize the election of all or a specified number of directors by the holders of one or more authorized classes of shares. A class (or classes) of shares entitled to elect one or more directors is a separate voting group for purposes of the election of directors. (1901, c. 2, ss. 14, 39; Rev., ss. 1147, 1182; C.S., ss. 1144, 1175; 1927, c. 138; G.S., ss. 55-48, 55-112; 1955, c. 1371, s. 1; 1959, c. 1316, s. 33; 1969, c. 751, ss. 10, 11; 1989, c. 265, s. 1.)

§ 55-8-05. Terms of directors generally.

(a) The terms of the initial directors of a corporation expire at the first shareholders' meeting at which directors are elected.

(b) The terms of all other directors expire at the next annual shareholders' meeting following their election unless their terms are staggered under G.S. 55-8-06.

(c) A decrease in the number of directors does not shorten an incumbent director's term.

(d) The term of a director elected to fill a vacancy expires at the next shareholders' meeting at which directors are elected.

(e) Despite the expiration of a director's term, he continues to serve until his successor is elected and qualifies or until there is a decrease in the number of directors. (1901, c. 2, ss. 14, 39; Rev., ss. 1147, 1182; C.S., ss. 1144, 1175; 1927, c. 138; G.S., ss. 55-48, 55-112; 1955, c. 1371, s. 1; 1959, c. 1316, s. 33; 1969, c. 751, ss. 10, 11; 1989, c. 265, s. 1.)

§ 55-8-06. Staggered terms for directors.

The articles of incorporation or bylaws adopted by the shareholders may provide for staggering the terms of directors by dividing the total number of directors into two, three, or four groups, with each group containing one-half, one-third, or one-fourth of the total, as near as may be. In that event, the terms of directors in the first group expire at the first annual shareholders' meeting after their election, the terms of the second group expire at the second annual shareholders' meeting after their election, the terms of the third group, if any, expire at the third annual shareholders' meeting after their election, and the terms of the fourth group, if any, expire at the fourth annual shareholders' meeting after their election. At each annual shareholders' meeting held thereafter, directors shall be chosen for a term of two, three, or four years, as the case may be, to succeed those whose terms expire. (1901, c. 2, ss. 14, 44; Rev., ss. 1147, 1148; C.S., s. 1144; 1937, c. 179; 1945, c. 200; 1949, c. 917; G.S., s. 55-48; 1955, c. 914, s. 1; c. 1371, s. 1; 1959, c. 1316, s. 7; 1989, c. 265, s. 1; 1993, c. 552, s. 10; 2005-268, s. 8.)

§ 55-8-07. Resignation of directors.

(a)   A director may resign at any time by communicating his resignation to the board of directors, its chair, or the corporation.

(b)   A resignation is effective when it is communicated unless it specifies in writing a later effective date or subsequent event upon which it will become effective. (1955, c. 1371, s. 1; 1959, c. 1316, s. 34; 1973, c. 469, s. 7; 1989, c. 265, s. 1; 2001-358, s. 6(c); 2001-387, ss. 173, 175(a); 2001-413, s. 6.)

§ 55-8-08. Removal of directors by shareholders.

(a)   The shareholders may remove one or more directors with or without cause unless the articles of incorporation provide that directors may be removed only for cause.

(b) If a director is elected by a voting group of shareholders, only the shareholders of that voting group may participate in the vote to remove him.

(c) If cumulative voting is authorized, unless the entire board of directors is to be removed, a director may not be removed if the number of votes sufficient to elect him under cumulative voting is voted against his removal. If cumulative voting is not authorized, a director may be removed only if the number of votes cast to remove him exceeds the number of votes cast not to remove him.

(d) A director may not be removed by the shareholders at a meeting unless the notice of the meeting states that the purpose, or one of the purposes, of the meeting is removal of the director.

(e) Unless otherwise provided in the articles of incorporation or a bylaw adopted by the shareholders, the entire board of directors may be removed from office with or without cause by the affirmative vote of a majority of the votes entitled to be cast at any election of directors. (1955, c. 1371, s. 1; 1959, c. 1316, s. 34; 1973, c. 469, s. 7; 1989, c. 265, s. 1; 1991, c. 645, s. 6.)

§ 55-8-09. Removal of directors by judicial proceeding.

(a) The superior court of the county where a corporation's principal office (or, if none in this State, its registered office) is located may remove a director of the corporation from office in a proceeding commenced either by the corporation or by its shareholders holding at least ten percent (10%) of the outstanding shares of any class if the court finds that:

(1) The director engaged in fraudulent or dishonest conduct, or gross abuse of authority or discretion, with respect to the corporation; and

(2) Removal is in the best interest of the corporation.

(b) The court that removes a director may bar the director from reelection for a period prescribed by the court.

(c) If shareholders commence a proceeding under subsection (a), they shall make the corporation a party defendant. (1955, c. 1371, s. 1; 1959, c. 1316, s. 34; 1973, c. 469, s. 7; 1989, c. 265, s. 1.)

§ 55-8-10. Vacancy on board.

(a) Unless the articles of incorporation provide otherwise, if a vacancy occurs on a board of directors, including, without limitation, a vacancy resulting from an increase in the number of directors or from the failure by the shareholders to elect the full authorized number of directors:

(1) The shareholders may fill the vacancy;

(2) The board of directors may fill the vacancy; or

(3) If the directors remaining in office constitute fewer than a quorum of the board, they may fill the vacancy by the affirmative vote of a majority of all the directors, or by the sole director, remaining in office.

(b) If the vacant office was held by a director elected by a voting group of shareholders, only the remaining director or directors elected by that voting group or the holders of shares of that voting group are entitled to fill the vacancy.

(c) A vacancy that will occur upon a specific later date or subsequent event (by reason of a resignation effective upon a later date or subsequent event under G.S. 55-8-07(b) or otherwise) may be filled before the vacancy occurs but the new director may not take office until the vacancy occurs. (1955, c. 1371, s. 1; 1959, c. 1316, s. 34; 1973, c. 469, s. 7; 1989, c. 265, s. 1; 1989 (Reg. Sess., 1990), c. 1024, s. 12.12.)

§ 55-8-11. Compensation of directors.

Unless the articles of incorporation or bylaws provide otherwise, the board of directors may fix the compensation of directors. (1955, c. 1371, s. 1; 1989, c. 265, s. 1.)

§§ 55-8-12 through 55-8-19. Reserved for future codification purposes.

Part 2. Meetings and Action of the Board.

§ 55-8-20. Meetings.

(a)   The board of directors may hold regular or special meetings in or out of this State.

(b)   Unless otherwise provided by the articles of incorporation, the bylaws or the board of directors, any or all directors may participate in a regular or special meeting by, or conduct the meeting through the use of, any means of communication by which all directors participating may simultaneously hear each other during the meeting. A director participating in a meeting by this means is deemed to be present in person at the meeting.

(c)   Unless the bylaws provide otherwise, special meetings of the board of directors may be called by the president or any two directors. (1955, c. 1371, s. 1; 1959, c. 1316, s. 8; 1969, c. 751, s. 12; 1973, c. 469, ss. 8-10; 1989, c. 265, s. 1; 1991, c. 645, s. 7.)

§ 55-8-21. Action without meeting.

(a)   Unless the articles of incorporation or bylaws provide otherwise, action required or permitted by this Chapter to be taken at a board of directors' meeting may be taken without a meeting if the action is taken by all members of the board. The action must be evidenced by one or more unrevoked written consents signed by each director before or after such action, describing the action taken, and included in the minutes or filed with the corporate records. To the extent the corporation has agreed pursuant to G.S. 55-1-50, a director's consent to action taken without meeting or revocation thereof may be in electronic form and delivered by electronic means.

(b)   Action taken under this section is effective when one or more unrevoked consents signed by all of the directors are delivered to the corporation, unless the consents specify a different effective date. A director's consent to action may be revoked in a writing signed by the director and delivered to the corporation prior to the action becoming effective.

(c) A consent signed under this section has the effect of a meeting vote and may be described as such in any document. (1955, c. 1371, s. 1; 1959, c. 1316, s. 8; 1969, c. 751, s. 12; 1973, c. 469, ss. 8-10; 1989, c. 265, s. 1; 2001-387, s. 15; 2005-268, s. 9.)

§ 55-8-22. Notice of meeting.

(a) Unless the articles of incorporation or bylaws provide otherwise, regular meetings of the board of directors may be held without notice of the date, time, place, or purpose of the meeting.

(b) Special meetings of the board of directors shall be held upon such notice as is provided in the articles of incorporation or bylaws, or in the absence of any such provision, upon notice sent by any usual means of communication not less than five days before the meeting. The notice need not describe the purpose of the special meeting unless required by this Chapter, the articles of incorporation or bylaws. (1955, c. 1371, s. 1; 1969, c. 751, s. 12; 1973, c. 469, s. 8; 1989, c. 265, s. 1.)

§ 55-8-23. Waiver of notice.

(a) A director may waive any notice required by this Chapter, the articles of incorporation, or bylaws before or after the date and time stated in the notice. Except as provided by subsection (b), the waiver must be in writing, signed by the director entitled to the notice, and filed with the minutes or corporate records.

(b) A director's attendance at or participation in a meeting waives any required notice to him of the meeting unless the director at the beginning of the meeting (or promptly upon his arrival) objects to holding the meeting or transacting business at the meeting and does not thereafter vote for or assent to action taken at the meeting. (1955, c. 1371, s. 1; 1969, c. 751, s. 12; 1973, c. 469, s. 8; 1989, c. 265, s. 1.)

§ 55-8-24. Quorum and voting.

(a) Unless the articles of incorporation or bylaws require a greater number, a quorum of a board of directors consists of:

(1) A majority of the fixed number of directors if the corporation has a fixed board size; or

(2) A majority of the number of directors prescribed, or if no number is prescribed the number in office immediately before the meeting begins, if the corporation has a variable-range size board.

(b) The articles of incorporation or a bylaw adopted by the shareholders may authorize a quorum of a board of directors to consist of no fewer than one-third of the fixed or prescribed number of directors determined under subsection (a).

(c) If a quorum is present when a vote is taken, the affirmative vote of a majority of directors present is the act of the board of directors unless the articles of incorporation or bylaws require the vote of a greater number of directors.

(d) A director who is present at a meeting of the board of directors or a committee of the board of directors when corporate action is taken is deemed to have assented to the action taken unless:

(1) He objects at the beginning of the meeting (or promptly upon his arrival) to holding it or transacting business at the meeting;

(2) His dissent or abstention from the action taken is entered in the minutes of the meeting; or

(3) He files written notice of his dissent or abstention with the presiding officer of the meeting before its adjournment or with the corporation immediately after adjournment of the meeting. The right of dissent or abstention is not available to a director who votes in favor of the action taken. (Code, s. 681; 1901, c. 2, ss. 33, 52; Rev., s. 1192; C.S., s. 1179; 1927, c. 121; 1933, c. 354, s. 1; G.S., s. 55-116; 1955, c. 1371, s. 1; 1959, c. 1316, s. 35; 1969, c. 751, s. 12; 1973, c. 469, s. 8; 1989, c. 265, s. 1.)

§ 55-8-25. Committees.

(a) Unless this Chapter, the articles of incorporation, or the bylaws provide otherwise, a board of directors may create one or more committees and appoint one or more members of the board of directors to serve on any such committee.

(b) Unless this Chapter provides otherwise, the creation of a committee and appointment of members to it must be approved by the greater of:

(1) A majority of all the directors in office when the action is taken; or

(2) The number of directors required by the articles of incorporation or bylaws to take action under G.S. 55-8-24.

(b1) The creation and appointment of a committee pursuant to G.S. 55-7-44(b)(2) may be approved in the manner set forth in G.S. 55-7-44(b)(2).

(c) G.S. 55-8-20 through G.S. 55-8-24 apply both to committees of the board of directors and to their members.

(d) To the extent specified by the board of directors or in the articles of incorporation or bylaws, each committee may exercise the authority of the board of directors under G.S. 55-8-01.

(e) A committee shall not, however, do any of the following:

(1) Authorize or approve distributions, except according to a formula or method, or within limits, prescribed by the board of directors.

(2) Approve or propose to shareholders action that this act requires be approved by shareholders.

(3) Fill vacancies on the board of directors or on any of its committees.

(4) Amend articles of incorporation pursuant to G.S. 55-10-02.

(5) Adopt, amend, or repeal bylaws.

(6) Approve a plan of merger not requiring shareholder approval.

(f) The creation of, delegation of authority to, or action by a committee does not alone constitute compliance by a director with the standards of conduct described in G.S. 55-8-30. (1955, c. 1371, s. 1; 1969, c. 751, s. 13; 1973, c. 1087, ss. 1, 2; 1989, c. 265, s. 1; 2005-268, s. 10; 2007-385, s. 1.)

§ 55-8-26. Submission of matters for shareholder vote.

A corporation may agree to submit a matter to a vote of its shareholders even if, after approving the matter, the board of directors determines it no longer recommends the matter. (2013-153, s. 7.)

§ 55-8-27: Reserved for future codification purposes.

§ 55-8-28: Reserved for future codification purposes.

§ 55-8-29: Reserved for future codification purposes.

Part 3. Standards of Conduct.

§ 55-8-30. General standards for directors.

(a) A director shall discharge his duties as a director, including his duties as a member of a committee:

(1) In good faith;

(2) With the care an ordinarily prudent person in a like position would exercise under similar circumstances; and

(3) In a manner he reasonably believes to be in the best interests of the corporation.

(b)   In discharging his duties a director is entitled to rely on information, opinions, reports, or statements, including financial statements and other financial data, if prepared or presented by:

(1)   One or more officers or employees of the corporation whom the director reasonably believes to be reliable and competent in the matters presented;

(2)   Legal counsel, public accountants, or other persons as to matters the director reasonably believes are within their professional or expert competence; or

(3)   A committee of the board of directors of which he is not a member if the director reasonably believes the committee merits confidence.

(c)   A director is not entitled to the benefit of subsection (b) if he has actual knowledge concerning the matter in question that makes reliance otherwise permitted by subsection (b) unwarranted.

(d)   A director is not liable for any action taken as a director, or any failure to take any action, if he performed the duties of his office in compliance with this section. The duties of a director weighing a change of control situation shall not be any different, nor the standard of care any higher, than otherwise provided in this section.

(e)   A director's personal liability for monetary damages for breach of a duty as a director may be limited or eliminated only to the extent permitted in G.S. 55-2-02(b)(3), and a director may be entitled to indemnification against liability and expenses pursuant to Part 5 of Article 8 of this Chapter. (1955, c. 1371, s. 1; 1989, c. 265, s. 1; 1993, c. 552, s. 11.)

§ 55-8-31. Director conflict of interest.

(a)   A conflict of interest transaction is a transaction with the corporation in which a director of the corporation has a direct or indirect interest. A conflict of interest transaction is not voidable by the corporation solely because of the director's interest in the transaction if any one of the following is true:

(1) The material facts of the transaction and the director's interest were disclosed or known to the board of directors or a committee of the board of directors and the board of directors or committee authorized, approved, or ratified the transaction;

(2) The material facts of the transaction and the director's interest were disclosed or known to the shareholders entitled to vote and they authorized, approved, or ratified the transaction; or

(3) The transaction was fair to the corporation.

(b) For purposes of this section, a director of the corporation has an indirect interest in a transaction if:

(1) Another entity in which he has a material financial interest or in which he is a general partner is a party to the transaction; or

(2) Another entity of which he is a director, officer, or trustee is a party to the transaction and the transaction is or should be considered by the board of directors of the corporation.

(c) For purposes of subsection (a)(1) of this section, a conflict of interest transaction is authorized, approved, or ratified if it receives the affirmative vote of a majority of the directors on the board of directors (or on the committee) who have no direct or indirect interest in the transaction. If a majority of the directors who have no direct or indirect interest in the transaction vote to authorize, approve, or ratify the transaction, a quorum is present for the purpose of taking action under this section. The presence of, or a vote cast by, a director with a direct or indirect interest in the transaction does not affect the validity of any action taken under subsection (a)(1) of this section if the transaction is otherwise authorized, approved, or ratified as provided in that subsection.

(d) For purposes of subsection (a)(2), a conflict of interest transaction is authorized, approved, or ratified if it receives the vote of a majority of the shares entitled to be counted under this subsection. Shares owned by or voted under the control of a director who has a direct or indirect interest in the transaction, and shares owned by or voted under the control of an entity described in subsection (b)(1), may not be counted in a vote of shareholders to determine whether to authorize, approve, or ratify a conflict of interest transaction under subsection (a)(2). The vote of those shares, however, shall be counted in determining whether the transaction is approved under other sections of this

Chapter. A majority of the shares that would if present be entitled to be counted in a vote on the transaction under this subsection constitutes a quorum for the purpose of taking action under this section. (1955, c. 1371, s. 1; 1989, c. 265, s. 1; 2005-268, s. 11.)

§ 55-8-32. Loans to directors.

(a)   Except as provided by subsection (c), a corporation may not directly or indirectly lend money to or guarantee the obligation of a director of the corporation unless:

(1)   The particular loan or guarantee is approved by a majority of the votes represented by the outstanding voting shares of all classes, voting as a single voting group, except the votes of shares owned by or voted under the control of the benefited director; or

(2)   The corporation's board of directors determines that the loan or guarantee benefits the corporation and either approves the specific loan or guarantee or a general plan authorizing loans and guarantees.

(b)   The fact that a loan or guarantee is made in violation of this section does not affect the borrower's liability on the loan.

(c)   This section does not apply to loans and guarantees authorized by statute regulating any special class of corporations.

(d)   For purposes of this section, a loan or guarantee is made indirectly to or for a director if such director has an indirect interest in the loan or guarantee as defined in G.S. 55-8-31 (b). (1955, c. 1371, s. 1; 1959, c. 1316, s. 6; 1961, c. 198; 1969, c. 751, s. 9; 1989, c. 265, s. 1.)

§ 55-8-33. Liability for unlawful distributions.

(a)   A director who votes for or assents to a distribution made in violation of G.S. 55-6-40 or the articles of incorporation is personally liable to the corporation for the amount of the distribution that exceeds what could have been distributed without violating G.S. 55-6-40 or the articles of incorporation if it is established that he did not perform his duties in compliance with G.S. 55-8-30. In any proceeding commenced under this section, a director has all of the defenses ordinarily available to a director.

(b)   A director held liable under subsection (a) for an unlawful distribution is entitled to:

(1)   Contribution from every other director who could be held liable under subsection (a) for the unlawful distribution; and

(2)   Reimbursement from each shareholder for the amount the shareholder accepted knowing the distribution was made in violation of G.S. 55-6-40 or the articles of incorporation.

(c)   A proceeding under subsection (a) is barred unless it is commenced within three years after the date on which the effect of the distribution was measured under G.S. 55-6-40(e) or (g). (Code, s. 681; 1901, c. 2, ss. 33, 52; Rev., s. 1192; C.S., s. 1179; 1927, c. 121; 1933, c. 354, s. 1; G.S., s. 55-116; 1955, c. 1371, s. 1; 1959, c. 1316, s. 35; 1989, c. 265, s. 1.)

§§ 55-8-34 through 55-8-39. Reserved for future codification purposes.

Part 4. Officers.

§ 55-8-40. Officers.

(a)   A corporation has the officers described in its bylaws or appointed by the board of directors in accordance with the bylaws.

(b)   A duly appointed officer may appoint one or more officers or assistant officers if authorized by the bylaws or the board of directors.

(c)   The secretary or any assistant secretary or any one or more other officers designated by the bylaws or the board of directors shall have the responsibility and authority to maintain and authenticate the records of the corporation.

(d) The same individual may simultaneously hold more than one office in a corporation, but no individual may act in more than one capacity where action of two or more officers is required.

(e) Whenever a specific office is referred to in this Chapter, it shall be deemed to include any individual who, alone or collectively with one or more other individuals, holds or occupies such office. (1901, c. 2, ss. 15, 16, 17; Rev., ss. 1149, 1150, 1151; C.S., s. 1145; G.S., s. 55-49; 1955, c. 1371, s. 1; 1959, c. 1316, s. 9; 1973, c. 1217; 1989, c. 265, s. 1; 1989 (Reg. Sess., 1990), c. 1024, s. 12.13.)

§ 55-8-41. Duties of officers.

Each officer has the authority and duties set forth in the bylaws or, to the extent consistent with the bylaws, the authority and duties prescribed by the board of directors or by direction of an officer authorized by the board of directors to prescribe the authority and duties of other officers. (1901, c. 2, ss. 15, 16, 17; Rev., ss. 1149, 1150, 1151; C.S., s. 1145; G.S., s. 55-49; 1955, c. 1371, s. 1; 1959, c. 1316, s. 9; 1973, c. 1217; 1989, c. 265, s. 1.)

§ 55-8-42. Standards of conduct for officers.

(a) An officer with discretionary authority shall discharge his duties under that authority:

(1) In good faith;

(2) With the care an ordinarily prudent person in a like position would exercise under similar circumstances; and

(3) In a manner he reasonably believes to be in the best interests of the corporation.

(b) In discharging his duties an officer is entitled to rely on information, opinions, reports, or statements, including financial statements and other financial data, if prepared or presented by:

(1) One or more officers or employees of the corporation whom the officer reasonably believes to be reliable and competent in the matters presented; or

(2) Legal counsel, public accountants, or other persons as to matters the officer reasonably believes are within their professional or expert competence.

(c) An officer is not entitled to the benefit of subsection (b) if he has actual knowledge concerning the matter in question that makes reliance otherwise permitted by subsection (b) unwarranted.

(d) An officer is not liable for any action taken as an officer, or any failure to take any action, if he performed the duties of his office in compliance with this section.

(e) An officer may be entitled to indemnification against liability and expenses pursuant to Part 5 of Article 8 of this Chapter. (1955, c. 1371, s. 1; 1989, c. 265, s. 1.)

§ 55-8-43. Resignation and removal of officers.

(a) An officer may resign at any time by communicating his resignation to the corporation. A resignation is effective when it is communicated unless it specifies in writing a later effective time. If a resignation is made effective at a later time and the corporation accepts the future effective time, its board of directors or the appointing officer may fill the pending vacancy before the effective time if the board of directors or the appointing officer provides that the successor does not take office until the effective time.

(b) An officer may be removed at any time with or without cause by (i) the board of directors, (ii) the appointing officer, unless the bylaws or the board of directors provide otherwise, or (iii) any other officer if authorized by the bylaws or the board of directors.

(c) In this section, "appointing officer" means the officer, including any successor to that officer, who appointed the officer resigning or being removed. (1901, c. 2, ss. 15, 16, 17; Rev., ss. 1149, 1150, 1151; C.S., s. 1145; G.S., s. 55-49; 1955, c. 1371, s. 1; 1959, c. 1316, s. 9; 1973, c. 1217; 1989, c. 265, s. 1; 2005-268, s. 12.)

§ 55-8-44. Contract rights of officers.

(a)   The appointment of an officer does not itself create contract rights.

(b)   An officer's removal does not itself affect the officer's contract rights, if any, with the corporation. An officer's resignation does not affect the corporation's contract rights, if any, with the officer. (1901, c. 2, ss. 15, 16, 17; Rev., ss. 1149, 1150, 1151; C.S., s. 1145; G.S., s. 55-49; 1955, c. 1371, s. 1; 1959, c. 1316, s. 9; 1973, c. 1217; 1989, c. 265, s. 1.)

§§ 55-8-45 through 55-8-49. Reserved for future codification purposes.

Part 5. Indemnification.

§ 55-8-50. Policy statement and definitions.

   (a) It is the public policy of this State to enable corporations organized under this Chapter to attract and maintain responsible, qualified directors, officers, employees and agents, and, to that end, to permit corporations organized under this Chapter to allocate the risk of personal liability of directors, officers, employees and agents through indemnification and insurance as authorized in this Part.

(b)   Definitions in this Part:

(1)   "Corporation" includes any domestic or foreign corporation absorbed in a merger which, if its separate existence had continued, would have had the obligation or power to indemnify its directors, officers, employees, or agents, so that a person who would have been entitled to receive or request indemnification from such corporation if its separate existence had continued shall stand in the same position under this Part with respect to the surviving corporation.

(2)   "Director" means an individual who is or was a director of a corporation or an individual who, while a director of a corporation, is or was serving at the

corporation's request as a director, officer, partner, trustee, employee, or agent of another foreign or domestic corporation, partnership, joint venture, trust, employee benefit plan, or other enterprise. A director is considered to be serving an employee benefit plan at the corporation's request if his duties to the corporation also impose duties on, or otherwise involve services by, him to the plan or to participants in or beneficiaries of the plan. "Director" includes, unless the context requires otherwise, the estate or personal representative of a director.

(3) "Expenses" means expenses of every kind incurred in defending a proceeding, including counsel fees.

(4) "Liability" means the obligation to pay a judgment, settlement, penalty, fine (including an excise tax assessed with respect to an employee benefit plan), or reasonable expenses incurred with respect to a proceeding.

(4a) "Officer", "employee", or "agent" includes, unless the context requires otherwise, the estate or personal representative of a person who acted in that capacity.

(5) "Official capacity" means: (i) when used with respect to a director, the office of director in a corporation; and (ii) when used with respect to an individual other than a director, as contemplated in G.S. 55-8-56, the office in a corporation held by the officer or the employment or agency relationship undertaken by the employee or agent on behalf of the corporation. "Official capacity" does not include service for any other foreign or domestic corporation or any partnership, joint venture, trust, employee benefit plan, or other enterprise.

(6) "Party" includes an individual who was, is, or is threatened to be made a named defendant or respondent in a proceeding.

(7) "Proceeding" means any threatened, pending, or completed action, suit, or proceeding, whether civil, criminal, administrative, or investigative and whether formal or informal. (1955, c. 1371, s. 1; 1969, c. 797, s. 2; 1973, c. 469, s. 6; 1985 (Reg. Sess., 1986), c. 1027, s. 39; 1989, c. 265, s. 1; 1993, c. 552, s. 12.)

§ 55-8-51. Authority to indemnify.

(a) Except as provided in subsection (d), a corporation may indemnify an individual made a party to a proceeding because he is or was a director against liability incurred in the proceeding if:

(1) He conducted himself in good faith; and

(2) He reasonably believed (i) in the case of conduct in his official capacity with the corporation, that his conduct was in its best interests; and (ii) in all other cases, that his conduct was at least not opposed to its best interests; and

(3) In the case of any criminal proceeding, he had no reasonable cause to believe his conduct was unlawful.

(b) A director's conduct with respect to an employee benefit plan for a purpose he reasonably believed to be in the interests of the participants in and beneficiaries of the plan is conduct that satisfies the requirement of subsection (a)(2)(ii).

(c) The termination of a proceeding by judgment, order, settlement, conviction, or upon a plea of no contest or its equivalent is not, of itself, determinative that the director did not meet the standard of conduct described in this section.

(d) A corporation may not indemnify a director under this section:

(1) In connection with a proceeding by or in the right of the corporation in which the director was adjudged liable to the corporation; or

(2) In connection with any other proceeding charging improper personal benefit to him, whether or not involving action in his official capacity, in which he was adjudged liable on the basis that personal benefit was improperly received by him.

(e) Indemnification permitted under this section in connection with a proceeding by or in the right of the corporation that is concluded without a final adjudication on the issue of liability is limited to reasonable expenses incurred in connection with the proceeding.

(f) The authorization, approval or favorable recommendation by the board of directors of a corporation of indemnification, as permitted by this section, shall not be deemed an act or corporate transaction in which a director has a conflict of interest, and no such indemnification shall be void or voidable on such ground. (1955, c. 1371, s. 1; 1969, c. 797, s. 2; 1973, c. 469, s. 6; 1985 (Reg. Sess., 1986), c. 1027, s. 39; 1989, c. 265, s. 1.)

§ 55-8-52. Mandatory indemnification.

Unless limited by its articles of incorporation, a corporation shall indemnify a director who was wholly successful, on the merits or otherwise, in the defense of any proceeding to which he was a party because he is or was a director of the corporation against reasonable expenses incurred by him in connection with the proceeding. (1955, c. 1371, s. 1; 1969, c. 797, ss. 2, 3; 1973, c. 469, s. 6; 1985 (Reg. Sess., 1986), c. 1027, ss. 39, 40; 1989, c. 265, s. 1.)

§ 55-8-53. Advance for expenses.

Expenses incurred by a director in defending a proceeding may be paid by the corporation in advance of the final disposition of such proceeding as authorized by the board of directors in the specific case or as authorized or required under any provision in the articles of incorporation or bylaws or by any applicable resolution or contract upon receipt of an undertaking by or on behalf of the director to repay such amount unless it shall ultimately be determined that he is entitled to be indemnified by the corporation against such expenses. (1955, c. 1371, s. 1; 1969, c. 797, s. 1; 1973, c. 469, s. 5; 1985 (Reg. Sess., 1986), c. 1027, ss. 35-38; 1989, c. 265, s. 1.)

§ 55-8-54. Court-ordered indemnification.

Unless a corporation's articles of incorporation provide otherwise, a director of the corporation who is a party to a proceeding may apply for indemnification to the court conducting the proceeding or to another court of competent jurisdiction. On receipt of an application, the court after giving any notice the court considers necessary may order indemnification if it determines:

(1) The director is entitled to mandatory indemnification under G.S. 55-8-52, in which case the court shall also order the corporation to pay the director's reasonable expenses incurred to obtain court-ordered indemnification; or

(2) The director is fairly and reasonably entitled to indemnification in view of all the relevant circumstances, whether or not he met the standard of conduct set forth in G.S. 55-8-51 or was adjudged liable as described in G.S. 55-8-51(d), but if he was adjudged so liable his indemnification is limited to reasonable expenses incurred. (1955, c. 1371, s. 1; 1969, c. 797, ss. 2, 3; 1973, c. 469, s. 6; 1985 (Reg. Sess., 1986), c. 1027, ss. 39, 40; 1989, c. 265, s. 1.)

§ 55-8-55. Determination and authorization of indemnification.

(a) A corporation may not indemnify a director under G.S. 55-8-51 unless authorized in the specific case after a determination has been made that indemnification of the director is permissible in the circumstances because he has met the standard of conduct set forth in G.S. 55-8-51.

(b) The determination shall be made:

(1) By the board of directors by majority vote of a quorum consisting of directors not at the time parties to the proceeding;

(2) If a quorum cannot be obtained under subdivision (1), by majority vote of a committee duly designated by the board of directors (in which designation directors who are parties may participate), consisting solely of two or more directors not at the time parties to the proceeding;

(3) By special legal counsel (i) selected by the board of directors or its committee in the manner prescribed in subdivision (1) or (2); or (ii) if a quorum of the board of directors cannot be obtained under subdivision (1) and a committee cannot be designated under subdivision (2), selected by majority vote of the full board of directors (in which selection directors who are parties may participate); or

(4) By the shareholders, but shares owned by or voted under the control of directors who are at the time parties to the proceeding may not be voted on the determination.

(c) Authorization of indemnification and evaluation as to reasonableness of expenses shall be made in the same manner as the determination that indemnification is permissible, except that if the determination is made by special legal counsel, authorization of indemnification and evaluation as to reasonableness of expenses shall be made by those entitled under subsection (b)(3) to select counsel. (1955, c. 1371, s. 1; 1969, c. 797, s. 2; 1973, c. 469, s. 6; 1985 (Reg. Sess., 1986), c. 1027, s. 39; 1989, c. 265, s. 1.)

§ 55-8-56. Indemnification of officers, employees, and agents.

Unless a corporation's articles of incorporation provide otherwise:

(1) An officer of the corporation is entitled to mandatory indemnification under G.S. 55-8-52, and is entitled to apply for court-ordered indemnification under G.S. 55-8-54, in each case to the same extent as a director;

(2) The corporation may indemnify and advance expenses under this Part to an officer, employee, or agent of the corporation to the same extent as to a director; and

(3) A corporation may also indemnify and advance expenses to an officer, employee, or agent who is not a director to the extent, consistent with public policy, that may be provided by its articles of incorporation, bylaws, general or specific action of its board of directors, or contract. (1955, c. 1371, s. 1; 1969, c. 797, s. 2; 1973, c. 469, s. 6; 1985 (Reg. Sess., 1986), c. 1027, s. 39; 1989, c. 265, s. 1.)

§ 55-8-57. Additional indemnification and insurance.

(a) In addition to and separate and apart from the indemnification provided for in G.S. 55-8-51, 55-8-52, 55-8-54, 55-8-55 and 55-8-56, a corporation may in its articles of incorporation or bylaws or by contract or resolution indemnify or agree to indemnify any one or more of its directors, officers, employees, or agents against liability and expenses in any proceeding (including without limitation a proceeding brought by or on behalf of the corporation itself) arising out of their status as such or their activities in any of the foregoing capacities; provided, however, that a corporation may not indemnify or agree to indemnify a person against liability or expenses he may incur on account of his activities which were at the time taken known or believed by him to be clearly in conflict with the best interests of the corporation. A corporation may likewise and to the same extent indemnify or agree to indemnify any person who, at the request of the corporation, is or was serving as a director, officer, partner, trustee, employee, or agent of another foreign or domestic corporation, partnership, joint venture, trust or other enterprise or as a trustee or administrator under an employee benefit plan. Any provision in any articles of incorporation, bylaw, contract, or resolution permitted under this section may include provisions for recovery from the corporation of reasonable costs, expenses, and attorneys' fees in connection with the enforcement of rights to indemnification granted therein and may further include provisions establishing reasonable procedures for determining and enforcing the rights granted therein.

(b) The authorization, adoption, approval, or favorable recommendation by the board of directors of a public corporation of any provision in any articles of incorporation, bylaw, contract or resolution, as permitted in this section, shall not be deemed an act or corporate transaction in which a director has a conflict of interest, and no such articles of incorporation or bylaw provision or contract or resolution shall be void or voidable on such grounds. The authorization, adoption, approval, or favorable recommendation by the board of directors of a nonpublic corporation of any provision in any articles of incorporation, bylaw, contract or resolution, as permitted in this section, which occurred prior to July 1, 1990, shall not be deemed an act or corporate transaction in which a director has a conflict of interest, and no such articles of incorporation, bylaw provision, contract or resolution shall be void or voidable on such grounds. Except as permitted in G.S. 55-8-31, no such bylaw, contract, or resolution not adopted, authorized, approved or ratified by shareholders shall be effective as to claims made or liabilities asserted against any director prior to its adoption, authorization, or approval by the board of directors.

(c) A corporation may purchase and maintain insurance on behalf of an individual who is or was a director, officer, employee, or agent of the corporation, or who, while a director, officer, employee, or agent of the corporation, is or was serving at the request of the corporation as a director, officer, partner, trustee, employee, or agent of another foreign or domestic corporation, partnership, joint venture, trust, employee benefit plan, or other enterprise, against liability asserted against or incurred by him in that capacity or arising from his status as a director, officer, employee, or agent, whether or not the corporation would have power to indemnify him against the same liability under any provision of this Chapter. (1955, c. 1371, s. 1; 1969, c. 797, s. 1;

1973, c. 469, s. 5; 1985 (Reg. Sess., 1986), c. 1027, ss. 35-38; 1989, c. 265, s. 1; 1989 (Reg. Sess., 1990), c. 1024, s. 12.14.)

§ 55-8-58. Application of Part.

(a) If articles of incorporation limit indemnification or advance for expenses, indemnification and advance for expenses are valid only to the extent consistent with the articles.

(b) This Part does not limit a corporation's power to pay or reimburse expenses incurred by a director in connection with his appearance as a witness in a proceeding at a time when he has not been made a named defendant or respondent to the proceeding.

(c) This Part shall not affect rights or liabilities arising out of acts or omissions occurring before July 1, 1990. (1989, c. 265, s. 1.)

Article 9.

Shareholder Protection Act.

§ 55-9-01. Short title and definitions.

(a) The provisions of this Article shall be known and may be cited as The North Carolina Shareholder Protection Act.

(b) In this Article:

(1) "Business combination" includes any merger, consolidation, or conversion of a corporation with or into any other corporation or any unincorporated entity, or the sale or lease of all or any substantial part of the corporation's assets to, or any payment, sale or lease to the corporation or any subsidiary thereof in exchange for securities of the corporation of any assets (except assets having an aggregate fair market value of less than five million dollars ($5,000,000)) of any other entity.

(2) "Common stock" means the shares of capital stock of the corporation that were not entitled to preference over any other shares, either in payment of dividends or in dissolution, at the time that the other entity acquired in excess of ten percent (10%) of the voting shares.

(3) "Continuing director" means a person who was a member of the board of directors of the corporation elected by the public shareholders prior to the time that the other entity acquired in excess of ten percent (10%) of the voting shares of the corporation, or a person recommended to succeed a continuing director by a majority of the continuing directors.

(4) "Exchange Act" means the act of Congress known as the Securities Exchange Act of 1934, as the same has been or hereafter may be amended from time to time.

(5) "Other consideration to be received" means, for the purposes of G.S. 55-9-03(1) and G.S. 55-9-03(2), the corporation's common stock retained by its existing public shareholders in the event of a business combination with the other entity in which the corporation is the surviving corporation.

(6) "Other entity" includes any domestic or foreign corporation, person or other form of entity and any such entity with which it or its "affiliate" or "associate" has an agreement, arrangement or understanding, directly or indirectly, for the purpose of acquiring, holding, voting or disposing of capital stock of the corporation, or which is its "affiliate" or "associate", as those terms are defined in the General Rules and Regulations under the Exchange Act, together with the successors and assigns of such persons in any transaction or series of transactions not involving a public offering of the corporation's capital stock within the meaning of the Securities Act of 1933, as amended.

(7) "Voting shares" means shares of the corporation's capital stock entitled to vote in the election of directors. (1987, c. 88, s. 1; c. 124, s. 1; 1989, c. 265, s. 1; 1999-369, s. 1.5; 2001-387, s. 16.)

§ 55-9-02. Voting requirement.

Notwithstanding any other provisions of the North Carolina Business Corporation Act, the affirmative vote of the holders of ninety-five percent (95%)

of the voting shares of a corporation, considered for the purposes of this section as one class, shall be required for the adoption or authorization of a business combination with any other entity if, as of the record date for the determination of shareholders entitled to notice thereof and to vote thereon, the other entity is the beneficial owner, directly or indirectly, of more than twenty percent (20%) of the voting shares of the corporation, considered for the purposes of this section as one class. (1987, c. 88. s. 1; 1989, c. 265, s. 1.)

§ 55-9-03. Exception to voting requirement.

The voting requirement of G.S. 55-9-02 shall not be applicable to a business combination if each of the following conditions is met:

(1) The cash, or fair market value of other consideration, to be received per share by the holders of the corporation's common stock in such business combination bears the same or a greater percentage relationship to the market price of the corporation's common stock immediately prior to the announcement of such business combination by the corporation as the highest per share price (including brokerage commissions and/or soliciting dealers' fees) which such other entity has theretofore paid for any of the shares of the corporation's common stock already owned by it bears to the market price of the corporation's common stock immediately prior to the commencement of acquisition of the corporation's common stock by such other entity, directly or indirectly;

(2) The cash, or fair market value of other consideration, to be received per share by holders of the corporation's common stock in such business combination (i) is not less than the highest per share price (including brokerage commissions and/or soliciting dealers' fees) paid by such other entity in acquiring any of its holdings of the shares of the corporation's common stock and (ii) is not less than the earnings per share of the corporation's common stock for the four full consecutive fiscal quarters immediately preceding the record date for the solicitation of votes on such business combination, multiplied by the then price/earnings multiple, if any, of such other entity as customarily computed and reported in the financial community;

(3) After the other entity has acquired a twenty percent (20%) interest and prior to the consummation of such business combination: (i) the other entity shall have taken steps to ensure that the corporation's board of directors included at all times representation by continuing directors proportionate to the

outstanding shares of the corporation's common stock held by persons not affiliated with the other entity (with a continuing director to occupy any resulting fractional board position); (ii) there shall have been no reduction in the rate of dividends payable on the corporation's common stock, except as may have been approved by a unanimous vote of its directors; (iii) the other entity shall have not acquired any newly issued shares of the corporation's capital stock, directly or indirectly, from the corporation, except upon conversion of any convertible securities acquired by the other entity prior to obtaining a twenty percent (20%) interest or as a result of a pro rata stock dividend or stock split; and (iv) the other entity shall not have acquired any additional shares of the corporation's outstanding common stock, or securities convertible into common stock, except as part of the transaction which resulted in the other entity acquiring its twenty percent (20%) interest;

(4)   The other entity shall not have (i) received the benefit, directly or indirectly, except proportionately with other shareholders, of any loans, advances, guarantees, pledges, or other financial assistance or tax credits provided by the corporation or (ii) made any major change in the corporation's business or equity capital structure unless by a unanimous vote of the directors, in either case prior to the consummation of the business combination; and

(5)   A proxy statement responsive to the requirements of the Exchange Act shall be mailed to the public shareholders of the corporation for the purpose of soliciting shareholder approval of the business combination and shall contain prominently in the forepart thereof any recommendations as to the advisability or inadvisability of the business combination which the continuing directors, or any of them, may choose to state and, if deemed advisable by a majority of the continuing directors, an opinion of a reputable investment banking firm as to the fairness (or not) of the terms of the business combination to the remaining public shareholders of the corporation, which investment banking firm shall be selected by a majority of the continuing directors and shall be paid by the corporation a reasonable fee for its services upon receipt of such opinion. (1987, c. 88, s. 1; 1989, c. 265, s. 1.)

§ 55-9-04. General.

(a)   The provisions of this Article shall also apply to a business combination with an other entity which at any time has been the beneficial owner, directly or indirectly, of more than twenty percent (20%) of the outstanding voting shares, considered for the purposes of this section as one class, notwithstanding that the other entity has reduced its percentage of shares below twenty percent (20%) if, as of the record date for the determination of shareholders entitled to notice of and to vote on the business combination, the other entity is an "affiliate" of the corporation.

(b)   For the purposes of the Article, an other entity shall be deemed the beneficial owner of any shares of the corporation's capital stock which the other entity has the right to acquire pursuant to any agreement, or upon exercise of any conversion rights, warrants or options, or otherwise (whether the right to acquire shares is exercisable immediately or only after the passage of time); and, further, the outstanding shares of any class of capital stock of the corporation shall include shares deemed beneficially owned through the application of the foregoing, but shall not include any other shares which may be issuable pursuant to any agreement, or upon exercise of any conversion rights, warrants or options, or otherwise.

(c)   A majority of the continuing directors shall have the power and duty to determine for the purposes of this Article on the basis of information known to them whether (i) an other entity beneficially owns more than twenty percent (20%) of the voting shares; (ii) an other entity is an "affiliate" or "associate" of another; (iii) an other entity has an agreement, arrangement or understanding with another; and (iv) the assets to be acquired by the corporation, or any subsidiary thereof, have an aggregate fair market value of less than five million dollars ($5,000,000).

(d)   Nothing contained in this Article shall be construed to relieve any other entity from any fiduciary obligation imposed by law. This Article shall be broadly construed so as to be applicable to any transaction reasonably calculated to avoid the application of the provisions hereof including, without limitation, any merger or other recapitalization, initiated by or for the benefit of an other entity that owns more than twenty percent (20%) of the voting shares, which would reincorporate a corporation under the laws of another state or which would reorganize a corporation as an unincorporated entity. (1987, c. 88, s. 1; 1989, c. 265, s. 1; 1999-369, s. 1.6.)

§ 55-9-05. Exemptions.

The provisions of G.S. 55-9-02 shall not be applicable to any corporation that shall be made the subject of a business combination by an other entity if: (i) the corporation was not a public corporation (as defined in G.S. 55-1-40(18a)) at the time such other entity acquired in excess of ten percent (10%) of the voting shares; (ii) on or before September 30, 1990 (or such earlier date as may be irrevocably established by resolution of the board of directors), the board of directors of a corporation to which G.S. 55-9-02 was not applicable on July 1, 1990, (other than a corporation described in G.S. 55-9-05(iii)) adopted a bylaw stating that the provisions of this Article shall not be applicable to the corporation; (iii) in the case of a corporation to which G.S. 55-9-02 was not applicable on July 1, 1990, as the result of adoption by its board of directors under G.S. 55-9-05(ii) of a bylaw providing that G.S. 55-9-02 not apply to such corporation, the board of directors of such corporation shall not have rescinded such bylaw on or before September 30, 1990 (or such earlier date as may be irrevocably established by resolution of the board of directors); (iv) in the case of a corporation (including its predecessors) which becomes a public corporation for the first time after July 1, 1990, such corporation adopts a bylaw within 90 days of becoming a public corporation stating that the provisions of this Article shall not be applicable to it; (v) in the case of a newly formed corporation after April 23, 1987, the initial articles of incorporation of the corporation shall provide that the provisions of this Article shall not be applicable; (vi) such business combination was the subject of an existing agreement of the corporation on April 23, 1987; or (vii) on or after September 1, 2000, and on or before December 31, 2000, the board of directors of a corporation to which G.S. 55-9-02 was applicable on September 1, 2000, adopts a bylaw stating that the provisions of this Article shall not be applicable to the corporation. Neither the adoption or failure to adopt a bylaw of the type set forth in G.S. 55-9-05(ii), (iv), or (vii) of this section nor the rescission or failure to rescind a bylaw of the type referred to in G.S. 55-9-05(iii) shall constitute grounds for any cause of action, at law or in equity, against the corporation or any of its directors. (1987, c. 88, s. 1; 1989, c. 265, s. 1; 1989 (Reg. Sess., 1990), c. 1024, s. 12.15; 2000-140, s. 44.)

Article 9A.

Control Share Acquisitions.

§ 55-9A-01. Short title and definitions.

(a) The provisions of this Article shall be known and may be cited as The North Carolina Control Share Acquisition Act.

(b) In this Article:

(1) "Beneficial ownership" of shares means the sole or shared ownership of any shares or the sole or shared power to vote any shares or to direct the exercise of voting power of any shares, whether such ownership or power is direct or indirect or through any contract, arrangement, understanding, relationship or otherwise, and includes shares beneficially owned by any person acting in concert with such beneficial owner pursuant to any contract, arrangement, understanding, relationship or otherwise. Notwithstanding the foregoing, beneficial ownership does not include shares acquired in the ordinary course of business for the benefit of others in good faith and not for the purpose of circumventing this Article, unless the acquiror of such shares may exercise or direct the exercise of voting of such shares without instruction from others.

(2) "Control shares" means shares of a covered corporation that when added to all other shares of the corporation beneficially owned by a person would entitle (except for this Article) that person to voting power in the election of directors that is equal to or greater than any of the following levels of voting power:

a. One-fifth of all voting power.

b. One-third of all voting power.

c. A majority of all voting power.

(3) "Control share acquisition" means the acquisition by any person of beneficial ownership of control shares, except that the acquisition of beneficial ownership of any shares of a covered corporation does not constitute a control share acquisition if the acquisition is consummated in any of the following circumstances:

a. Before April 30, 1987.

b. Pursuant to a contract existing before April 30, 1987, with either:

(i) The covered corporation; or

(ii) A seller of such shares who owned such shares before April 30, 1987.

c. Pursuant to the laws of descent and distribution.

d. Pursuant to the satisfaction of a pledge or other security interest created in good faith and not for the purpose of circumventing this Article.

e. Pursuant to a transaction effected in compliance with applicable law, but only if the transaction is pursuant to an agreement to which the covered corporation is a party.

f. Pursuant to the sale of such shares by the covered corporation or its parent or subsidiary corporation.

g. Pursuant to a written agreement to which the covered corporation is a party that permits the purchasers of shares from the covered corporation or its parent or subsidiary corporation also to purchase in any manner within 90 days before or after the purchase from the covered corporation or its parent or subsidiary up to the same aggregate number of shares as were sold by the covered corporation or its parent or subsidiary corporation.

h. By an employee benefit plan established by the covered corporation.

i. Before the corporation became a covered corporation.

For purposes of this definition, shares acquired within any consecutive 90-day period or shares acquired pursuant to a plan to make a control share acquisition are considered to have been acquired in the same acquisition.

(4) "Interested shares" means the shares of a covered corporation beneficially owned by any of the following persons:

a. Any person who has acquired or proposes to acquire control shares in a control share acquisition.

b. Any officer of the covered corporation.

c. Any employee of the covered corporation who is also a director of the corporation.

(5) "Covered corporation" means a corporation that:

a. Is incorporated under the laws of North Carolina and has substantial assets within North Carolina;

b. Has a class of shares registered under Section 12 of the Securities Exchange Act of 1934;

c. Has its principal place of business or principal office within North Carolina; and

d. Has either:

(i) More than ten percent (10%) of its shareholders resident in North Carolina; or

(ii) More than ten percent (10%) of its shares owned by North Carolina residents.

(6) The residence of a shareholder is presumed to be the address appearing in the records of the corporation.

(7) For purposes of calculating the percentages or numbers described in subsection (b)(5) of this section, any shares held in trust or by a nominee shall be deemed to be held by the beneficiaries of such trust or by the beneficiaries of such shares held by such nominee. (1987, c. 182, s. 1; 1989, c. 200, s. 1; c. 265, s. 1; 1989 (Reg. Sess., 1990), c. 1024, s. 12.16; 2001-201, s. 16.)

§ 55-9A-02. Acquiring person statement.

Any person who has made a control share acquisition or who has made a bona fide written offer to make a control share acquisition may at the person's election deliver an acquiring person statement to the covered corporation at the covered corporation's principal office. The acquiring person statement must set forth all of the following:

(1) The identity of the acquiring person and each other beneficial owner of shares that are beneficially owned by the acquiring person.

(2) A statement that the acquiring person statement is given pursuant to this Article.

(3) The number of shares of the covered corporation beneficially owned by the acquiring person and each other beneficial owner named under subdivision (1) of this section.

(4) The level of voting power above which the control share acquisition falls or would, if consummated, fall.

(5) If the control share acquisition has not taken place:

a. A description in reasonable detail of the terms of the proposed control share acquisition; and

b. Representations of the acquiring person, together with a statement in reasonable detail of the facts upon which they are based, that the proposed control share acquisition, if consummated, will not be contrary to law, and that the acquiring person has the financial capacity to make the proposed control share acquisition. (1987, c. 182, s. 1; 1989, c. 200, s. 1, c. 265, s. 1.)

§ 55-9A-03. Meeting of shareholders.

(a) If the acquiring person so requests at the time of delivery of an acquiring person statement and gives an undertaking to pay the covered corporation's expenses of a special meeting, within 10 days after delivery of such request the directors of the covered corporation shall call a special meeting of shareholders of the covered corporation for the purpose of considering the voting rights to be accorded the control shares acquired or to be acquired in the control share acquisition.

(b) Unless the acquiring person agrees in writing to another date, the special meeting of shareholders shall be held within 50 days after the receipt by the covered corporation of the request.

(c) If no request is made, the voting rights to be accorded the control shares acquired in the control share acquisition shall be considered at the next special or annual meeting of shareholders.

(d) If the acquiring person so requests in writing at the time of delivery of the acquiring person statement, the special meeting must not be held sooner than 30 days after receipt by the covered corporation of the acquiring person statement. (1987, c. 182, s. 1; 1989, c. 265, s. 1.)

§ 55-9A-04. Notice.

If a special meeting is requested pursuant to G.S. 55-9A-03, notice of the special meeting of shareholders shall be given as promptly as reasonably practicable by the covered corporation. Notice of any special or annual meeting at which the voting rights of control shares are to be considered shall be given to all shareholders who are entitled to vote at the meeting and who are shareholders of record as of the record date set for the meeting, and to all holders of interested shares, and such notice must include or be accompanied by each of the following:

(1) A copy of the acquiring person statement delivered to the covered corporation pursuant to this Article.

(2) A statement by the board of directors of the covered corporation, authorized by a majority of its directors, of its position or recommendation, or that it is taking no position or making no recommendation, with respect to granting voting rights to the control shares acquired or proposed to be acquired in the control share acquisition.

(3) If the shareholders would have a right of redemption under G.S. 55-9A-06, a statement, displayed with reasonable prominence, describing such right and advising the shareholders that it will be available only to those who give the written notice required by G.S. 55-9A-06(b). (1987, c. 182, s. 1; 1989, c. 200, s. 1, c. 265, s. 1.)

§ 55-9A-05. Voting rights.

(a) Control shares acquired in a control share acquisition shall not have voting rights unless such rights are granted by resolution adopted by the shareholders of the covered corporation.

(b) To be approved under this section, the resolution must be adopted by the affirmative vote of the holders of at least a majority of all the outstanding shares of the covered corporation (not including interested shares) entitled to vote for the election of directors; provided that if applicable law or an articles of incorporation or bylaw provision adopted by the shareholders before the occurrence of the control share acquisition that is the subject of the vote prescribes voting by separate classes of shares, the resolution must also be adopted by the affirmative vote of the holders of at least a majority of each such class (but excluding in any such case all interested shares); and provided further that if applicable law or an articles of incorporation or bylaw provision adopted by the shareholders before the occurrence of the control share acquisition that is the subject of the vote prescribes voting by shares that would not otherwise be entitled to vote, such shares shall be treated solely for purposes of this section as shares entitled to vote for directors (but excluding in any such case all interested shares). (1987, c. 182, s. 1; 1989, c. 265, s. 1.)

§ 55-9A-06. Right of redemption by shareholders.

(a) Unless otherwise provided in the articles of incorporation or a bylaw of the covered corporation adopted by the shareholders before a control share acquisition has occurred and subject to G.S. 55-6-40, if control shares acquired in a control share acquisition are accorded voting rights and the holders of the control shares have a majority of all voting power for the election of directors, all shareholders of the covered corporation (other than holders of control shares) have rights as prescribed in this section to have their shares redeemed by the corporation at the fair value of those shares as of the day prior to the date on which the vote was taken under G.S. 55-9A-05.

(b) If the notice of meeting at which voting rights are accorded to control shares contains the statement required by G.S. 55-9A-04(3), a shareholder will not have any right of redemption under this section unless he gives to the corporation, prior to or at the meeting of shareholders at which the voting rights to be accorded to control shares are considered, written notice that if voting rights are accorded to such shares he may ask for the redemption of his shares hereunder.

(c) As soon as practicable after control shares held by persons having a majority of all voting power for the election of directors have been accorded voting rights, the board of directors shall cause a notice to be sent to all shareholders of the corporation advising them of the facts and that if they gave the notice required by subsection (b) of this section they may have rights to have their shares redeemed at the fair value of those shares pursuant to this section.

(d) Within 30 days after the date on which a shareholder receives such notice, such shareholder may make written demand on the corporation for payment of the fair value of his shares, and after such demand, if such shareholder has complied with the notice requirement in subsection (b) of this section, the corporation shall redeem his shares at their fair value within 30 days after the date on which the corporation receives such shareholder's written demand for payment.

(e) As used in this section, "fair value" means a value not less than the highest price paid per share by the acquiring person in the control share acquisition. (1987, c. 182, s. 1; 1989, c. 200, s. 1, c. 265, s. 1.)

§ 55-9A-07. Severability.

If any provision or clause of this Article or application thereof to any person or circumstance is held invalid, such invalidity shall not affect other provisions or applications of this Article that can be given effect without the invalid provision or application, and to this end the provisions of this Article are declared to be severable. (1987, c. 182, s. 1; 1989, c. 265, s. 1.)

§ 55-9A-08. Construction.

The provisions of this Article shall apply notwithstanding any provisions of Article 7 of this Chapter and in the event of any conflict between this Article and Article 7, the provisions of this Article shall control. (1989, c. 265, s. 1.)

§ 55-9A-09. Exemptions.

The provisions of this Article shall not be applicable to any corporation if, on or before September 30, 1990, or such earlier date as may be irrevocably established by resolution of the board of directors, or at any time before the corporation becomes, or after it ceases to be, a covered corporation, the board of directors adopts a bylaw stating that the provisions of this Article shall not be applicable to the corporation; or, in the case of a corporation formed after August 12, 1987, its initial articles of incorporation provide that this Article shall not be applicable to the corporation; or on or after September 1, 2000, and on or before December 31, 2000, the board of directors of a corporation to which the provisions of this Article were applicable on September 1, 2000, adopts a bylaw stating that the provisions of this Article shall not be applicable to the corporation. Neither adoption nor failure to adopt such a bylaw or provision shall constitute grounds for any cause of action against the corporation, or any officer or director of the corporation. (1987, c. 773, s. 12; 1989, c. 200, s. 1; c. 265, s. 1; 2000-140, s. 47.)

Article 10.

Amendment of Articles of Incorporation and Bylaws.

Part 1. Amendment of Articles of Incorporation.

§ 55-10-01. Authority to amend.

(a) A corporation may amend its articles of incorporation at any time to add or change a provision that is required or permitted in the articles of incorporation or to delete a provision not required in the articles of incorporation. Whether a provision is required or permitted in the articles of incorporation is determined as of the effective date of the amendment.

(b) A shareholder of the corporation does not have a vested property right resulting from any provision in the articles of incorporation, including provisions relating to management, control, capital structure, dividend entitlement, or purpose or duration of the corporation. (1901, c. 2, ss. 29,30,37; 1903, c. 510; Rev., ss. 1175, 1178; C.S., s. 1131; 1927, c. 142, G.S., s. 55-31; 1955, c. 1371, s. 1; 1959, c. 1316, s. 29; 1989, c. 265, s. 1.)

§ 55-10-02. Amendment by board of directors.

Unless the articles of incorporation provide otherwise, a corporation's board of directors may adopt any of the following amendments to the corporation's articles of incorporation without shareholder approval:

(1)   Reserved for future codification purposes.

(2)   To delete the names and addresses of the initial directors.

(3)   To delete the name and address of the initial registered agent or registered office, if a statement of change is on file with the Secretary of State.

(4)   If the corporation has only one class of shares outstanding:

a.   To change each issued and unissued authorized share of the class into a greater number of whole shares of the class; or

b.   To increase the number of authorized shares of the class to the extent necessary to permit the issuance of shares as a share dividend.

(5)   To change the corporate name by substituting the word "corporation", "incorporated", "company", "limited", or the abbreviation "corp.", "inc.", "co.", or "ltd.", for a similar word or abbreviation in the name, or by adding, deleting, or changing a geographical attribution for the name.

(5a)   To reflect a reduction in authorized shares pursuant to G.S. 55-6-31(b) when the corporation has acquired its own shares and the articles of incorporation prohibit the reissue of the acquired shares.

(5b)   To delete a class of shares from the articles of incorporation, as a result of the operation of G.S. 55-6-31(b), when there are no remaining authorized shares of the class because the corporation has acquired all authorized shares of the class and the articles of incorporation prohibit the reissue of the acquired shares.

(6)   To make any other change expressly permitted by this Chapter to be made without shareholder approval. (1893, c. 380; 1899, c. 618; 1901, c. 2, ss. 28, 29, 30, 37; 1903, c. 510; Rev., ss. 1174, 1175, 1178; C.S., ss. 1130, 1131; 1925, c. 118, ss. 1, 2a; 1927, c. 142; 1931, c. 243, ss. 4, 5; 1933, c. 100, ss. 7, 8; 1941, c. 97, s. 5; G.S., ss. 55-30, 55-31; 1953, c. 54; c. 119, ss. 1, 2; 1955, c. 1371, s. 1; 1959, c. 1316, s. 25; 1973, c. 469, s. 30; 1989, c. 265, s. 1; 2005-268, s. 13.)

§ 55-10-03. Amendment by board of directors and shareholders.

(a)   If a corporation has issued shares, an amendment to the articles of incorporation shall be adopted pursuant to this section. Except as provided in G.S. 55-14A-01, the proposed amendment must be adopted by the board of directors.

(b)   Except as provided in G.S. 55-10-02, 55-10-07, and 55-14A-01, after adopting the proposed amendment the board of directors shall submit the amendment to the shareholders for their approval. The board of directors shall also transmit to the shareholders a recommendation that the shareholders approve the amendment, unless one of the following circumstances exist, in which event the board of directors shall communicate the basis for not recommending approval of the amendment to the shareholders at the time it submits the amendment to the shareholders:

(1)   The board of directors determines that, because of conflict of interest or other special circumstances, it should not make a recommendation that the shareholders approve the amendment.

(2)   G.S. 55-8-26 applies.

(c)   The board of directors may condition its submission of the amendment to the shareholders on any basis.

(d)   If the amendment must be approved by the shareholders and the approval is to be given at a meeting, the corporation must notify each shareholder in accordance with G.S. 55-7-05, whether or not the shareholder is entitled to vote, of the meeting of shareholders at which the amendment is to be submitted for approval. The notice of meeting must state that the purpose, or one of the purposes, of the meeting is to consider the amendment and the notice must contain or be accompanied by a copy or summary of the amendment. If the amendment is required to be approved by the shareholders and the approval is to be obtained through action without meeting, the corporation must notify shareholders if required by G.S. 55-7-04(d).

(e)   Unless this Chapter, the articles of incorporation, a bylaw adopted by the shareholders, or the board of directors (acting pursuant to subsection (c)) require a greater vote or a vote by voting groups, the amendment to be adopted must be approved by all of the following:

(1)　A majority of the votes entitled to be cast on the amendment by any voting group with respect to which the amendment would create appraisal rights.

(2)　The votes required by G.S. 55-7-25 and G.S. 55-7-26 by every other voting group entitled to vote on the amendment. (1893, c. 380; 1899, c. 618; 1901, c. 2, ss. 28, 29, 30, 37; 1903, c. 510; Rev., ss. 1174, 1175, 1178; C.S., ss. 1130, 1131; 1925, c. 118, ss. 1, 2a; 1927, c. 142; 1931, c. 243, ss. 4, 5; 1933, c. 100, ss. 7, 8; 1941, c. 97, s. 5; G.S., ss. 55-30, 55-31; 1953, c. 54; c. 119, ss. 1, 2; 1955, c. 1371, s. 1; 1959, c. 1316, s. 25; 1973, c. 469, s. 30; 1989, c. 265, s. 1; 1991, c. 645, s. 8; 2000-140, s. 101(b); 2005-268, s. 14; 2011-347, s. 5; 2013-153, s. 8.)

§ 55-10-04. Voting on amendments by voting groups.

(a)　The holders of the outstanding shares of a class are entitled to vote as a separate voting group (if shareholder voting is otherwise required by this Chapter) on a proposed amendment if the amendment would:

(1)　Increase or decrease the aggregate number of authorized shares of the class;

(2)　Effect an exchange or reclassification of all or part of the shares of the class into shares of another class;

(3)　Effect an exchange or reclassification, or create the right of exchange, of all or part of the shares of another class into shares of the class;

(4)　Change the designation, rights, preferences, or limitations of all or part of the shares of the class;

(5)　Change the shares of all or part of the class into a different number of shares of the same class;

(6) Create a new class of shares having rights or preferences with respect to distributions or to dissolution that are prior, superior, or substantially equal to the shares of the class;

(7) Increase the rights, preferences, or number of authorized shares of any class that, after giving effect to the amendment, have rights or preferences with respect to distributions or to dissolution that are prior, superior, or substantially equal to the shares of the class;

(8) Limit or deny an existing preemptive right of all or part of the shares of the class;

(9) Cancel or otherwise affect rights to distributions or dividends that have accumulated but not yet been declared on all or part of the shares of the class; or

(10) Change the corporation into a nonprofit corporation or a cooperative organization.

(b) If a proposed amendment would affect a series of a class of shares in one or more of the ways described in subsection (a), the shares of that series are entitled to vote as a separate voting group on the proposed amendment.

(c) If a proposed amendment that entitles two or more series of shares to vote as separate voting groups under this section would affect those two or more series in the same or a substantially similar way, the shares of all the series so affected must vote together as a single voting group on the proposed amendment.

(d) A class or series of shares is entitled to the voting rights granted by this section although the articles of incorporation provide that the shares are nonvoting shares. (1955, c. 1371, s. 1; 1959, c. 1316, ss. 30, 31; 1969, c. 751, s. 36; 1989, c. 265, s. 1.)

§ 55-10-05. Amendment before issuance of shares.

If a corporation has not yet issued shares, the board of directors, or if the corporation has no directors, a majority of the incorporators may adopt one or more amendments to the corporation's articles of incorporation. (1893, c. 380;

1899, c. 618; 1901, c. 2, ss. 28, 29, 30, 37; 1903, c. 510; Rev., ss. 1174, 1175, 1178; C.S., ss. 1130, 1131; 1925, c. 118, ss. 1, 2a; 1927, c. 142; 1931, c. 243, ss. 4, 5; 1933, c. 100, ss. 7, 8; 1941, c. 97, s. 5; G.S., ss. 55-30, 55-31; 1953, c. 54; c. 119, ss. 1, 2; 1955, c. 1371, s. 1; 1959, c. 1316, s. 25; 1973, c. 469, s. 30; 1989, c. 265, s. 1; 1991, c. 645, s. 9.)

§ 55-10-06. Articles of amendment.

A corporation amending its articles of incorporation shall deliver to the Secretary of State for filing articles of amendment setting forth:

(1)   The name of the corporation;

(2)   The text of each amendment adopted;

(3)   If an amendment provides for an exchange, reclassification, or cancellation of issued shares, provisions for implementing the amendment if not contained in the amendment itself;

(4)   The date of each amendment's adoption;

(5)   If an amendment was adopted by the incorporators or board of directors without shareholder action, a statement to that effect and a brief explanation of why shareholder action was not required;

(6)   If an amendment was approved by the shareholders, a statement that shareholder approval was obtained as required by this Chapter. (1955, c. 1371, s. 1; 1959, c. 1316, s. 32; 1989, c. 265, s. 1; 1991, c. 645, s. 10(a).)

§ 55-10-07. Restated articles of incorporation.

(a)   A corporation's board of directors may restate its articles of incorporation at any time, with or without shareholder approval, to consolidate all amendments into a single document.

(b)   The restated articles of incorporation may include one or more new amendments to the articles. If the restated articles of incorporation include a new amendment requiring shareholder approval, it must be adopted and approved as provided in G.S. 55-10-03. The restated articles of incorporation may include a statement of the address of the current registered office and the name of the current registered agent of the corporation, and no other.

(c)   Repealed by Session Laws 2005, c. 268, s. 15.

(d)   A corporation restating its articles of incorporation shall deliver to the Secretary of State for filing articles of restatement which shall:

(1)   Set forth the name of the corporation;

(2)   Attach as an exhibit thereto the text of the restated articles of incorporation;

(3)   State that the restated articles of incorporation consolidate all amendments into a single document; and

(4)   If the restated articles of incorporation contain a new amendment to the articles, include the statements required by G.S. 55-10-06.

(e)   Duly adopted restated articles of incorporation supersede the original articles of incorporation and all amendments to the original articles of incorporation.

(f)   The Secretary of State may certify restated articles of incorporation as the articles of incorporation currently in effect without including the other information required by subsection (d) of this section. (1955, c. 1371, s. 1; 1989, c. 265, s. 1; 1991, c. 645, ss. 11, 18; 2005-268, s. 15.)

§ 55-10-08. Reserved for future codification purposes.

§ 55-10-09. Effect of amendment.

An amendment to articles of incorporation does not affect a cause of action existing against or in favor of the corporation, a proceeding to which the corporation is a party, or the existing rights of persons other than shareholders of the corporation. An amendment changing a corporation's name does not abate a proceeding brought by or against the corporation in its former name. (1955, c. 1371, s. 1; 1989, c. 265, s. 1.)

§§ 55-10-10 through 55-10-19. Reserved for future codification purposes.

Part 2. Amendment of Bylaws.

§ 55-10-20. Amendment by board of directors or shareholders.

(a) A corporation's board of directors may amend or repeal the corporation's bylaws, except to the extent otherwise provided in the articles of incorporation or a bylaw adopted by the shareholders or this Chapter, and except that a bylaw adopted, amended or repealed by the shareholders may not be readopted, amended or repealed by the board of directors if neither the articles of incorporation nor a bylaw adopted by the shareholders authorizes the board of directors to adopt, amend or repeal that particular bylaw or the bylaws generally.

(b) A corporation's shareholders may amend or repeal the corporation's bylaws even though the bylaws may also be amended or repealed by its board of directors. (1955, c. 1371, s. 1; 1959, c. 1316, ss. 2, 3; 1973, c. 469, s. 4; 1989, c. 265, s. 1.)

§ 55-10-21. Reserved for future codification purposes.

§ 55-10-22. Bylaw increasing quorum or voting requirement for directors.

(a) A bylaw that fixes a greater quorum or voting requirement for the board of directors may be amended or repealed:

(1) If originally adopted by the shareholders, only by the shareholders, unless amendment or repeal by the board of directors is permitted pursuant to subsection (b);

(2) If originally adopted by the board of directors, either by the shareholders or by the board of directors.

(b) A bylaw adopted or amended by the shareholders that fixes a greater quorum or voting requirement for the board of directors may provide that it may be amended or repealed only by a specified vote of either the shareholders or the board of directors.

(c) A bylaw referred to in subsection (a):

(1) May not be adopted by the board of directors by a vote less than a majority of the directors then in office, and

(2) May not itself be amended by a quorum or vote of the directors less than the quorum or vote therein prescribed or prescribed by the shareholders pursuant to subsection (b). (1955, c. 1371, s. 1; 1959, c. 1316, ss. 2, 3; 1973, c. 469, s. 4; 1989, c. 265, s. 1.)

Article 11.

Merger and Share Exchange.

§ 55-11-01. Merger.

(a) One or more corporations may merge into another corporation if the board of directors of each corporation adopts and its shareholders (if required by G.S. 55-11-03) approve a plan of merger.

(b) The plan of merger must set forth:

(1) The name of each corporation planning to merge and the name of the surviving corporation into which each other corporation plans to merge;

(2) The terms and conditions of the merger; and

(3) The manner and basis of converting the shares of each corporation into shares, obligations, or other securities of the surviving or any other corporation or into cash or other property in whole or part.

(c) The plan of merger may set forth:

(1) Amendments to the articles of incorporation of the surviving corporation; and

(2) Other provisions relating to the merger.

(d) The provisions of the plan of merger, other than the provisions referred to in subdivisions (b)(1) and (c)(1) of this section, may be made dependent on facts objectively ascertainable outside the plan of merger if the plan of merger sets forth the manner in which the facts will operate upon the affected provisions. The facts may include any of the following:

(1) Statistical or market indices, market prices of any security or group of securities, interest rates, currency exchange rates, or similar economic or financial data.

(2) A determination or action by the corporation or by any other person, group, or body.

(3) The terms of, or actions taken under, an agreement to which the corporation is a party, or any other agreement or document. (1925, c. 77, s. 1; 1939, c. 5; 1943, c. 270; G.S., s. 55-165; 1955, c. 1371, s. 1; 1969, c. 751, s. 37; 1973, c. 469, s. 31; 1989, c. 265, s. 1; 2005-268, s. 16.)

§ 55-11-02. Share exchange.

(a) A corporation may acquire all of the outstanding shares of one or more classes or series of another corporation if the board of directors of each corporation adopts and its shareholders (if required by G.S. 55-11-03) approve the exchange.

(b) The plan of exchange must set forth:

(1) The name of the corporation whose shares will be acquired and the name of the acquiring corporation;

(2) The terms and conditions of the exchange;

(3) The manner and basis of exchanging the shares to be acquired for shares, obligations, or other securities of the acquiring or any other corporation or for cash or other property in whole or part.

(c) The plan of exchange may set forth other provisions relating to the exchange.

(c1) The provisions of the plan of share exchange, other than the provision required by subdivision (b)(1) of this section, may be made dependent on facts objectively ascertainable outside the plan of share exchange if the plan of share exchange sets forth the manner in which the facts will operate upon the affected provisions. The facts may include any of the following:

(1) Statistical or market indices, market prices of any security or group of securities, interest rates, currency exchange rates, or similar economic or financial data.

(2) A determination or action by the corporation or by any other person, group, or body.

(3) The terms of, or actions taken under, an agreement to which the corporation is a party, or any other agreement or document.

(d) This section does not limit the acquisition of all or part of the shares of one or more classes or series of a corporation through a voluntary exchange or otherwise. (1989, c. 265, s. 1; 2005-268, s. 17.)

§ 55-11-03. Action on plan.

(a) After adopting a plan of merger or share exchange, the board of directors of each corporation party to the merger, and the board of directors of the corporation whose shares will be acquired in the share exchange, shall submit the plan of merger (except as provided in subsection (g)) or share exchange for approval by its shareholders.

(b) The following requirements shall be met for a plan of merger or share exchange to be approved:

(1) The board of directors shall recommend to the shareholders that the plan of merger or share exchange be approved, unless one of the following circumstances exist, in which event the board of directors shall communicate the basis for not recommending approval of the plan of merger or share exchange to the shareholders at the time it submits the plan of merger or share exchange to the shareholders:

a. The board of directors determines that, because of conflict of interest or other special circumstances, it should not make a recommendation that the shareholders approve the plan of merger or share exchange.

b. G.S. 55-8-26 applies.

(2) The shareholders entitled to vote must approve the plan of merger or share exchange.

(c) The board of directors may condition its submission of the proposed merger or share exchange on any basis.

(d) The corporation shall notify each shareholder, whether or not entitled to vote, of the proposed shareholders' meeting in accordance with G.S. 55-7-05. The notice must state that the purpose, or one of the purposes, of the meeting is to consider the plan of merger or share exchange and contain or be accompanied by a copy or summary of the plan.

(e) Unless this Chapter, the articles of incorporation, a bylaw adopted by the shareholders, or the board of directors (acting pursuant to subsection (c)) require a greater vote, the plan of merger or share exchange to be authorized must be approved by each voting group entitled to vote separately on the plan by a majority of all the votes entitled to be cast on the plan by that voting group and, for the purpose of Article 9 or any provision in the articles of incorporation or bylaws adopted prior to July 1, 1990, a merger shall be deemed to include a share exchange. If any shareholder of a merging corporation has or will have personal liability for any existing or future obligation of the surviving corporation in the merger solely as a result of owning one or more shares in the surviving corporation, then, in addition to the requirements of this subsection, authorization of the plan of merger by the merging corporation shall require the affirmative vote or written consent of that shareholder.

(f)   Separate voting by voting groups is required for the following:

(1)   On a plan of merger if the plan contains a provision that, if contained in a proposed amendment to articles of incorporation, would require action by one or more separate voting groups on the proposed amendment under G.S. 55-10-04, except where the consideration to be received in exchange for the shares of that group consists solely of cash.

(2)   On a plan of share exchange by each class or series of shares to be acquired in the exchange, with each class or series constituting a separate voting group.

(g)   Unless the articles of incorporation provide otherwise, approval by the surviving corporation's shareholders of a plan of merger is not required if all of the following conditions are met:

(1)   Except for amendments permitted by G.S. 55-10-02, its articles of incorporation will not be changed.

(2)   Each shareholder of the corporation whose shares were outstanding immediately before the effective date of the merger will hold the same shares, with identical preferences, limitations, and relative rights, immediately after the effective date of the merger.

(3)   The number of voting shares outstanding immediately after the merger, plus the number of voting shares issuable as a result of the merger (either by the conversion of securities issued pursuant to the merger or the exercise of rights and warrants issued pursuant to the merger), will not exceed by more than twenty percent (20%) the total number of voting shares of the surviving corporation outstanding immediately before the merger.

(4)   The number of participating shares outstanding immediately after the merger, plus the number of participating shares issuable as a result of the merger (either by the conversion of securities issued pursuant to the merger or the exercise of rights and warrants issued pursuant to the merger), will not exceed by more than twenty percent (20%) the total number of participating shares outstanding immediately before the merger.

(h) As used in subsection (g):

(1) "Participating shares" means shares that entitle their holders to participate without limitation in distributions.

(2) "Voting shares" means shares that entitle their holders to vote unconditionally in elections of directors.

(i) After a plan of merger or share exchange is authorized, but before the articles of merger or share exchange become effective, the plan of merger or share exchange (i) may be amended as provided in the plan of merger or share exchange, or (ii) may be abandoned, subject to any contractual rights, as provided in the plan of merger or share exchange or, if there is no such provision, as determined by the board of directors without further shareholder action. (1925, c. 77, s. 1; 1939, c. 5; 1943, c. 270; G.S., s. 55-165; 1955, c. 1371, s. 1; 1959, c. 1316, s. 37; 1973, c. 469, s. 33; 1989, c. 265, s. 1; 1989 (Reg. Sess., 1990), c. 1024, s. 12.17; 1993, c. 552, s. 14; 2005-268, ss. 18, 19, 20; 2013-153, s. 9.)

§ 55-11-04. Merger between parent and subsidiary or between subsidiaries.

(a) Subject to Article 9, a parent corporation owning shares of a domestic or foreign subsidiary corporation that carry at least ninety percent (90%) of the voting power of each class and series of the outstanding shares of the subsidiary corporation that have the current power to vote in the election of directors may merge the subsidiary into itself or into another such subsidiary without approval of the shareholders of the parent corporation unless the articles of incorporation of the parent corporation require approval of the shareholders or the plan of merger contains one or more amendments to the articles of incorporation of the parent corporation for which shareholder approval is required by G.S. 55-10-03, and without approval of the board of directors or shareholders of the subsidiary corporation unless the articles of incorporation of the subsidiary corporation require approval of the shareholders of the subsidiary corporation, or if the subsidiary is a foreign corporation, approval by the subsidiary's board of directors or shareholders is required by the laws under which the subsidiary is organized. Subject to Article 9, a parent corporation owning shares of a domestic or foreign subsidiary corporation that carry at least ninety percent (90%) of the voting power of each class and series of the outstanding shares of the subsidiary corporation that have the current power to vote in the election of directors may merge itself into the subsidiary corporation without approval of the board of directors or shareholders of the subsidiary corporation unless the articles of incorporation of the subsidiary corporation provide otherwise, the plan of merger contains one or more amendments to the articles of incorporation of the subsidiary corporation for which shareholder approval is required by G.S. 55-10-03, or, if the subsidiary is a foreign corporation, approval by the subsidiary's board of directors or shareholders is required by the laws under which the subsidiary is organized. Except as otherwise provided in this subsection, the provisions of G.S. 55-11-01 and G.S. 55-11-03 apply to any merger described in this subsection.

(b)   If a merger is consummated without approval of the subsidiary corporation's shareholders, the surviving corporation shall, within 10 days after the effective date of the merger, notify each shareholder of the subsidiary corporation as of the effective date of the merger, that the merger has become effective.

(c)   Repealed by Session Laws 2005, c. 268, s. 21.

(d)   Repealed by Session Laws 2005, c. 268, s. 21.

(e)   Repealed by Session Laws 2005, c. 268, s. 21.

(f)   The provisions of G.S. 55-13-02(b) do not apply to subsidiary corporations that are parties to mergers consummated under this section. (1955, c. 1371, s. 1; 1959, c. 1316, s. 37; 1973, c. 469, s. 33; 1989, c. 265, s. 1; 1997-485, s. 29; 2005-268, s. 21; 2006-226, s. 16(a); 2013-153, s. 10.)

§ 55-11-05. Articles of merger or share exchange.

(a)   After a plan of merger or a plan of share exchange for the acquisition of shares of a domestic corporation has been authorized as required by this Chapter, the surviving or acquiring corporation shall deliver to the Secretary of State for filing articles of merger or share exchange.

In the case of a merger, the articles of merger shall set forth (i) the name and state or country of incorporation of each merging corporation, (ii) the name of the merging corporation that will survive the merger and, if the surviving corporation is not authorized to transact business or conduct affairs in this State, a designation of its mailing address and a commitment to file with the Secretary of State a statement of any subsequent change in its mailing address, (iii) any amendments to the articles of incorporation of the surviving corporation provided in the plan of merger if the surviving corporation is a domestic corporation, and (iv) a statement that the plan of merger has been approved by each merging corporation in the manner required by law.

In the case of a share exchange, the articles of share exchange shall set forth (i) the name of the corporation whose shares will be acquired, (ii) the name and state or country of incorporation of the acquiring corporation, (iii) a designation of its mailing address and a commitment to file with the Secretary of State a statement of any subsequent change in its mailing address if the acquiring corporation is not authorized to transact business or conduct affairs in this State, and (iv) a statement that the plan of share exchange has been approved by the corporation whose shares will be acquired and by the acquiring corporation in the manner required by law.

(a1) If the plan of merger or share exchange is amended after the articles of merger or share exchange have been filed but before the articles of merger or share exchange become effective and any statement in the articles of merger or share exchange becomes incorrect as a result of the amendment, the surviving or acquiring corporation shall deliver to the Secretary of State for filing prior to the time the articles of merger or share exchange become effective an amendment to the articles of merger or share exchange correcting the incorrect statement. If the articles of merger or share exchange are abandoned after the articles of merger or share exchange are filed but before the articles of merger or share exchange become effective, the surviving or acquiring corporation shall deliver to the Secretary of State for filing prior to the time the articles of merger or share exchange become effective an amendment reflecting abandonment of the plan of merger or share exchange.

(b) A merger or share exchange takes effect when the articles of merger or share exchange become effective.

(c) Certificates of merger shall also be registered as provided in G.S. 47-18.1.

(d) In the case of a merger pursuant to G.S. 55-11-07 or a share exchange pursuant to G.S. 55-11-07, references in subsections (a) and (a1) of this section to "corporation" shall include a domestic corporation, a domestic nonprofit corporation, a foreign corporation, and a foreign nonprofit corporation as applicable. (1925, c. 77, s. 1; 1939, c. 5; 1943, c. 270; G.S., s. 55-165; 1955, c. 1371, s. 1; 1967, c. 823, s. 18; 1973, c. 469, s. 34; 1989, c. 265, s. 1; 1991, c. 645, s. 10(b); 2005-268, s. 22; 2006-226, s. 16(b); 2006-259, s. 14.5(a)-(b); 2006-264, s. 44(b).)

§ 55-11-06. Effect of merger or share exchange.

(a)   When a merger pursuant to G.S. 55-11-01, 55-11-04, 55-11-07, or 55-11-09 takes effect:

(1)   Each other merging corporation merges into the surviving corporation and the separate existence of each merging corporation except the surviving corporation ceases.

(2)   The title to all real estate and other property owned by each merging corporation is vested in the surviving corporation without reversion or impairment.

(3)   The surviving corporation has all liabilities of each merging corporation.

(4)   A proceeding pending by or against any merging corporation may be continued as if the merger did not occur or the surviving corporation may be substituted in the proceeding for a merging corporation whose separate existence ceases in the merger.

(5)   If a domestic corporation survives the merger, its articles of incorporation are amended to the extent provided in the articles of merger.

(6)   The shares of each merging corporation that are to be converted into shares, obligations, or other securities of the surviving or any other corporation or into the right to receive cash or other property are thereupon converted, and the former holders of the shares are entitled only to the rights provided to them in the plan of merger or, in the case of former holders of shares in a domestic corporation, any right they may have under Article 13 of this Chapter.

(7)   If a foreign corporation or foreign nonprofit corporation survives the merger, it is deemed:

a. To agree that it will promptly pay to shareholders of any merging domestic corporation exercising appraisal rights the amount, if any, to which they are entitled under Article 13 of this Chapter and otherwise to comply with the requirements of Article 13 as if it were a surviving domestic corporation in the merger.

b. To agree that it may be served with process in this State in any proceeding for enforcement (i) of any obligation of any merging domestic corporation, (ii) of the appraisal rights of shareholders of any merging domestic corporation under Article 13 of this Chapter, and (iii) of any obligation of the surviving foreign corporation or foreign nonprofit corporation arising from the merger.

c. To have appointed the Secretary of State as its agent for service of process in any proceeding for enforcement as specified in sub-subdivision b. of this subdivision. Service of process on the Secretary of State shall be made by delivering to, and leaving with, the Secretary of State, or with any clerk authorized by the Secretary of State to accept service of process, duplicate copies of the process and the fee required by G.S. 55-1-22(b). Upon receipt of service of process on behalf of a surviving foreign corporation or foreign nonprofit corporation in the manner provided for in this section, the Secretary of State shall immediately mail a copy of the process by registered or certified mail, return receipt requested, to the surviving foreign corporation or foreign nonprofit corporation. If the surviving foreign corporation or foreign nonprofit corporation is authorized to transact business or conduct affairs in this State, the address for mailing shall be its principal office designated in the latest document filed with the Secretary of State that is authorized by law to designate the principal office, or, if there is no principal office on file, its registered office. If the surviving foreign corporation or foreign nonprofit corporation is not authorized to transact business or conduct affairs in this State, the address for mailing shall be the mailing address designated pursuant to G.S. 55-11-05(a).

(b) When a share exchange for the acquisition of shares of a domestic corporation pursuant to G.S. 55-11-02 or G.S. 55-11-07 takes effect:

(1) The shares of the acquired corporation are exchanged as provided in the plan of share exchange, and the former holders of the shares are entitled only to the exchange rights provided in the plan of share exchange or any right they may have under Article 13 of this Chapter.

(2)   If the acquiring corporation is not a domestic corporation, it is deemed to agree that it will promptly pay to shareholders of the acquired corporation exercising appraisal rights the amount, if any, to which they are entitled under Article 13 of this Chapter and otherwise to comply with the requirements of Article 13 as if it were an acquiring domestic corporation in the share exchange.

(3)   If the acquiring corporation is not a domestic corporation, the acquiring corporation is deemed:

a.   To agree that it may be served with process in this State in any proceeding for enforcement (i) of the appraisal rights of shareholders of the acquired corporation under Article 13 of this Chapter and (ii) of any obligation of the acquiring corporation arising from the share exchange; and

b.   To have appointed the Secretary of State as its agent for service of process in any proceeding for enforcement as specified in sub-subdivision a. of this subdivision. Service of process on the Secretary of State shall be made by delivering to, and leaving with, the Secretary of State, or with any clerk authorized by the Secretary of State to accept service of process, duplicate copies of the process and the fee required by G.S. 55-1-22(b). Upon receipt of service of process on behalf of an acquiring corporation in the manner provided for in this section, the Secretary of State shall immediately mail a copy of the process by registered or certified mail, return receipt requested, to the acquiring corporation. If the acquiring corporation is authorized to transact business or conduct affairs in this State, the address for mailing shall be its principal office designated in the latest document filed with the Secretary of State that is authorized by law to designate the principal office or, if there is no principal office on file, its registered office. If the acquiring corporation is not authorized to transact business or conduct affairs in this State, the address for mailing shall be the mailing address designated pursuant to G.S. 55-11-05(a).

(c)   In the case of a merger pursuant to G.S. 55-11-07 or G.S. 55-11-09 or a share exchange pursuant to G.S. 55-11-07, references in subsections (a) and (b) of this section to "corporation " shall include a domestic corporation, a domestic nonprofit corporation, a foreign corporation, and a foreign nonprofit corporation as applicable. (1925, c. 77, s. 1; 1943, c. 270; G.S., s. 55-166; 1955, c. 1371, s. 1; 1967, c. 950, s. 1; 1989, c. 265, s. 1; 1999-369, s. 1.7; 2005-268, s. 23; 2006-264, s. 44(c); 2011-347, ss. 6, 7.)

§ 55-11-07. Merger or share exchange with foreign corporation.

(a)   One or more foreign corporations may merge with one or more domestic corporations, and a foreign corporation may enter into a share exchange with a domestic corporation if:

(1)   In a merger, the merger is permitted by the law of the state or country under whose law each foreign corporation is incorporated and, to the extent applicable, each domestic or foreign corporation complies with that law in effecting the merger;

(2)   In a share exchange, if the corporation whose shares will be acquired is a foreign corporation, the share exchange is permitted by the law of the state or country under whose law the foreign corporation is incorporated and the foreign corporation and the acquiring domestic corporation comply with that law in effecting the share exchange;

(3)   The foreign corporation complies with G.S. 55-11-05 if it is the surviving corporation of the merger or acquiring corporation of the share exchange; and

(4)   Each domestic corporation complies with the applicable provisions of G.S. 55-11-01 through G.S. 55-11-04 and, if it is the surviving corporation of the merger with G.S. 55-11-05.

(b)   Repealed by Session Laws 2005, c. 268, s. 24.

(c)   This section does not limit the power of a foreign corporation to acquire all or part of the shares of one or more classes or series of a domestic corporation through a voluntary exchange or otherwise, or the power of a domestic corporation to acquire all or part of the shares of one or more classes or series of a foreign corporation through a voluntary exchange or otherwise. (1925, c. 77, s. 1; 1939, c. 5; 1943, c. 270; G.S., s. 55-165; 1955, c. 1371, s. 1; 1973, c. 469, s. 35; 1989, c. 265, s. 1; 2001-387, ss. 18, 19; 2005-268, s. 24.)

§ 55-11-08. Article 9 to control.

Nothing in this Article shall be construed to modify in any manner the provisions or applicability of Article 9. (1989, c. 265, s. 1.)

§ 55-11-09. Merger with nonprofit corporation.

(a) One or more domestic or foreign nonprofit corporations may merge with one or more domestic corporations if:

(1) Each domestic nonprofit corporation complies with the applicable provisions of G.S. 55A-11-01 through G.S. 55A-11-03;

(2) In a merger involving one or more foreign nonprofit corporations, the merger is permitted by law of the state or country under whose law each foreign nonprofit corporation is incorporated and, to the extent applicable, each domestic corporation and each domestic or foreign nonprofit corporation complies with that law in effecting the merger;

(3) The domestic or foreign nonprofit corporation complies with G.S. 55-11-05 if it is the surviving corporation; and

(4) Each domestic corporation complies with the applicable provisions of G.S. 55-11-01, 55-11-03, and 55-11-04 and, if it is the surviving corporation, with G.S. 55-11-05.

(b) Repealed by Session Laws 2005, c. 268, s. 25.

(c) This section does not limit the power of a domestic or foreign nonprofit corporation to acquire all or part of the shares of one or more classes or series of a domestic corporation through a voluntary exchange or otherwise. (1995, c. 400, s. 13; 2001-387, ss. 20, 21; 2005-268, s. 25.)

§ 55-11-10. Merger with unincorporated entity.

(a) Repealed by Session Laws 2001-387, s. 22, effective January 1, 2002.

(b) One or more domestic corporations may merge with one or more unincorporated entities and, if desired, one or more foreign corporations, domestic nonprofit corporations, or foreign nonprofit corporations if:

(1) The merger is permitted by the laws of the state or country governing the organization and internal affairs of each other merging business entity; and

(2) Each merging domestic corporation and each other merging business entity comply with the requirements of this section and, to the extent applicable, the laws referred to in subdivision (1) of this subsection.

(c) Each merging domestic corporation and each other merging business entity shall approve a written plan of merger containing:

(1) For each merging business entity, its name, type of business entity, and the state or country whose laws govern its organization and internal affairs;

(2) The name of the merging business entity that shall survive the merger;

(3) The terms and conditions of the merger;

(4) The manner and basis for converting the interests in each merging business entity into interests, obligations, or securities of the surviving business entity or into cash or other property in whole or in part; and

(5) If the surviving business entity is a domestic corporation, any amendments to its articles of incorporation that are to be made in connection with the merger.

(c1) The plan of merger may contain other provisions relating to the merger.

(c2) The provisions of the plan of merger, other than the provisions referred to in subdivisions (1), (2), and (5) of subsection (c) of this section, may be made dependent on facts objectively ascertainable outside the plan of merger if the plan of merger sets forth the manner in which the facts will operate upon the affected provisions. The facts may include any of the following:

(1) Statistical or market indices, market prices of any security or group of securities, interest rates, currency exchange rates, or similar economic or financial data.

(2) A determination or action by the corporation or by any other person, group, or body.

(3) The terms of, or actions taken under, an agreement to which the corporation is a party, or any other agreement or document.

(c3) In the case of a domestic corporation, approval of the plan of merger requires that the plan of merger be adopted by its board of directors as provided in G.S. 55-11-03 and, unless shareholder approval is not required under subsection (g) of G.S. 55-11-03, be approved by its shareholders as provided in G.S. 55-11-03. If any shareholder of a merging domestic corporation has or will have personal liability for any existing or future obligation of the surviving business entity solely as a result of holding an interest in the surviving business entity, then in addition to the requirements of the preceding sentence, approval of the plan of merger by the domestic corporation shall require the affirmative vote or written consent of that shareholder. In the case of each other merging business entity, the plan of merger must be approved in accordance with the laws of the state or country governing the organization and internal affairs of that merging business entity.

(c4) After a plan of merger has been approved by a domestic corporation but before the articles of merger become effective, the plan of merger (i) may be amended as provided in the plan of merger, or (ii) may be abandoned (subject to any contractual rights) as provided in the plan of merger or, if there is no such provision, as determined by the board of directors without further shareholder action.

(d) After a plan of merger has been approved by each merging domestic corporation and each other merging business entity as provided in subsection (c) of this section, the surviving business entity shall deliver articles of merger to the Secretary of State for filing. The articles of merger shall set forth all of the following:

(1) Repealed by Session Laws 2005, c. 268, s. 27.

(2) For each merging business entity, its name, type of business entity, and the state or country whose laws govern its organization and internal affairs.

(3) The name of the merging business entity that shall survive the merger and, if the surviving business entity is not authorized to transact business or conduct affairs in this State, a designation of its mailing address and a commitment to file with the Secretary of State a statement of any subsequent change in its mailing address.

(3a) If the surviving business entity is a domestic corporation, any amendment to its articles of incorporation as provided in the plan of merger.

(4) A statement that the plan of merger has been approved by each merging business entity in the manner required by law.

(5) Repealed by Session Laws 2005, c. 268, s. 27.

If the plan of merger is amended after the articles of merger have been filed but before the articles of merger become effective, and any statement in the articles of merger becomes incorrect as a result of the amendment, the surviving business entity shall deliver to the Secretary of State for filing prior to the time the articles of merger become effective an amendment to the articles of merger correcting the incorrect statement. If the articles of merger are abandoned after the articles of merger are filed but before the articles of merger become effective, the surviving business entity shall deliver to the Secretary of State for filing prior to the time the articles of merger become effective an amendment reflecting abandonment of the plan of merger.

Certificates of merger shall also be registered as provided in G.S. 47-18.1.

(e) A merger takes effect when the articles of merger become effective. When a merger takes effect:

(1) Each other merging business entity merges into the surviving business entity and the separate existence of each merging business entity except the surviving business entity ceases;

(2) The title to all real estate and other property owned by each merging business entity is vested in the surviving business entity without reversion or impairment;

(3) The surviving business entity has all liabilities of each merging business entity;

(4) A proceeding pending by or against any merging business entity may be continued as if the merger did not occur, or the surviving business entity may be substituted in the proceeding for a merging business entity whose separate existence ceases in the merger;

(5) If a domestic corporation is the surviving business entity, its articles of incorporation shall be amended to the extent provided in the articles of merger;

(6) The interests in each merging business entity that are to be converted into interests, obligations, or securities of the surviving business entity or into the right to receive cash or other property are thereupon so converted, and the former holders of the interests are entitled only to the rights provided to them in the plan of merger or, in the case of former holders of shares in a domestic corporation, any rights they may have under Article 13 of this Chapter; and

(7) If the surviving business entity is not a domestic corporation, the surviving business entity is deemed to agree that it will promptly pay to the shareholders of any merging domestic corporation exercising appraisal rights the amount, if any, to which they are entitled under Article 13 of this Chapter and otherwise to comply with the requirements of Article 13 as if it were a surviving domestic corporation in the merger.

The merger shall not affect the liability or absence of liability of any holder of an interest in a merging business entity for any acts, omissions, or obligations of any merging business entity made or incurred prior to the effectiveness of the merger. The cessation of separate existence of a merging business entity in the merger shall not constitute a dissolution or termination of the merging business entity.

(e1) If the surviving business entity is not a domestic limited liability company, a domestic corporation, a domestic nonprofit corporation, or a domestic limited partnership, when the merger takes effect the surviving business entity is deemed:

(1) To agree that it may be served with process in this State in any proceeding for enforcement (i) of any obligation of any merging domestic limited liability company, domestic corporation, domestic nonprofit corporation, domestic limited partnership, or other partnership as defined in G.S. 59-36 that is formed under the laws of this State, (ii) the appraisal rights of shareholders of any merging domestic corporation under Article 13 of this Chapter, and (iii) any obligation of the surviving business entity arising from the merger; and

(2) To have appointed the Secretary of State as its agent for service of process in any such proceeding. Service on the Secretary of State of any such process shall be made by delivering to and leaving with the Secretary of State, or with any clerk authorized by the Secretary of State to accept service of

process, duplicate copies of such process and the fee required by G.S. 55-1-22(b). Upon receipt of service of process on behalf of a surviving business entity in the manner provided for in this section, the Secretary of State shall immediately mail a copy of the process by registered or certified mail, return receipt requested, to the surviving business entity. If the surviving business entity is authorized to transact business or conduct affairs in this State, the address for mailing shall be its principal office designated in the latest document filed with the Secretary of State that is authorized by law to designate the principal office or, if there is no principal office on file, its registered office. If the surviving business entity is not authorized to transact business or conduct affairs in this State, the address for mailing shall be the mailing address designated pursuant to subdivision (3) of subsection (d) of this section.

(f) This section does not apply to a merger that does not include a merging unincorporated entity. (1999-369, s. 1.8; 2000-140, s. 45; 2001-387, ss. 22, 23, 24, 25; 2005-268, ss. 26, 27, 28; 2007-385, s. 2; 2011-347, ss. 8, 9.)

Article 11A.

Conversions.

Part 1. Conversion to Corporation.

§ 55-11A-01. Conversion.

A business entity, other than a domestic corporation, may convert to a domestic corporation if:

(1) The conversion is permitted by the laws of the state or country governing the organization and internal affairs of the converting business entity; and

(2) The converting business entity complies with the requirements of this Part and, to the extent applicable, the laws referred to in subdivision (1) of this section. (2001-387, s. 17.)

§ 55-11A-02. Plan of conversion.

(a) The converting business entity shall approve a written plan of conversion containing:

(1) The name of the converting business entity, its type of business entity, and the state or country whose laws govern its organization and internal affairs;

(2) The name of the resulting domestic corporation into which the converting business entity shall convert;

(3) The terms and conditions of the conversion; and

(4) The manner and basis for converting the interests in the converting business entity into shares, obligations, or other securities of the resulting domestic corporation or into cash or other property in whole or in part.

(a1) The plan of conversion may contain other provisions relating to the conversion.

(a2) The provisions of the plan of conversion, other than the provisions required by subdivisions (1) and (2) of subsection (a) of this section, may be made dependent on facts objectively ascertainable outside the plan of conversion if the plan of conversion sets forth the manner in which the facts will operate upon the affected provisions. The facts may include any of the following:

(1) Statistical or market indices, market prices of any security or group of securities, interest rates, currency exchange rates, or similar economic or financial data.

(2) A determination or action by the converting business entity or by any other person, group, or body.

(3) The terms of, or actions taken under, an agreement to which the converting business entity is a party, or any other agreement or document.

(b) The plan of conversion shall be approved in accordance with the laws of the state or country governing the organization and internal affairs of the converting business entity.

(c) After a plan of conversion has been approved as provided in subsection (b) of this section, but before articles of incorporation for the resulting domestic corporation become effective, the plan of conversion may be amended or abandoned to the extent permitted by the laws that govern the organization and internal affairs of the converting business entity. (2001-387, s. 17; 2005-268, s. 29.)

§ 55-11A-03. Filing of articles of incorporation by converting entity.

(a) After a plan of conversion has been approved by the converting business entity as provided in G.S. 55-11A-02, the converting business entity shall deliver articles of incorporation to the Secretary of State for filing. In addition to the matters required or permitted by G.S. 55-2-02, the articles of incorporation shall contain articles of conversion stating:

(1) That the corporation is being formed pursuant to a conversion of a business entity;

(2) The name of the converting business entity, its type of business entity, and the state or country whose laws govern its organization and internal affairs; and

(3) That a plan of conversion has been approved by the converting business entity as required by law.

(b) If the plan of conversion is abandoned after the articles of incorporation have been filed with the Secretary of State but before the articles of incorporation become effective, the converting business entity shall deliver to the Secretary of State for filing prior to the time the articles of incorporation become effective an amendment to the articles of incorporation withdrawing the articles of incorporation.

(c) The conversion takes effect when the articles of incorporation become effective.

(d) Certificates of conversion shall also be registered as provided in G.S. 47-18.1. (2001-387, s. 17.)

§ 55-11A-04. Effects of conversion.

When the conversion takes effect:

(1)   The converting business entity ceases its prior form of organization and continues in existence as the resulting domestic corporation;

(2)   The title to all real estate and other property owned by the converting business entity continues vested in the resulting domestic corporation without reversion or impairment;

(3)   All liabilities of the converting business entity continue as liabilities of the resulting domestic corporation;

(4)   A proceeding pending by or against the converting business entity may be continued as if the conversion did not occur; and

(5)   The interests in the converting business entity that are to be converted into shares, obligations, or other securities of the resulting domestic corporation or into the right to receive cash or other property are thereupon so converted, and the former holders of interests in the converting business entity are entitled only to the rights provided in the plan of conversion.

The conversion shall not affect the liability or absence of liability of any holder of an interest in the converting business entity for any acts, omissions, or obligations of the converting business entity made or incurred prior to the effectiveness of the conversion. The cessation of the existence of the converting business entity in its prior form of organization in the conversion shall not constitute a dissolution or termination of the converting business entity. (2001-387, s. 17.)

§§ 55-11A-05 through 55-11A-09. Reserved for future codification purposes.

Part 2. Conversion of Corporation.

§ 55-11A-10. Conversion.

A domestic corporation may convert to a different business entity if:

(1)　The conversion is permitted by the laws of the state or country governing the organization and internal affairs of such other business entity; and

(2)　The converting domestic corporation complies with the requirements of this Part and, to the extent applicable, the laws referred to in subdivision (1) of this section. (2001-387, s. 17.)

§ 55-11A-11. Plan of conversion.

(a)　The converting domestic corporation shall approve a written plan of conversion containing all of the following:

(1)　The name of the converting domestic corporation.

(2)　The name of the resulting business entity into which the domestic corporation shall convert, its type of business entity, and the state or country whose laws govern its organization and internal affairs.

(3)　The terms and conditions of the conversion.

(4)　The manner and basis for converting the shares of the domestic corporation into interests, obligations, or securities of the resulting business entity or into cash or other property in whole or in part.

(a1)　The plan of conversion may contain other provisions relating to the conversion.

(a2)　The provisions of the plan of conversion, other than the provisions required by subdivisions (1) and (2) of subsection (a) of this section, may be made dependent on facts objectively ascertainable outside the plan of conversion if the plan of conversion sets forth the manner in which the facts will operate upon the affected provisions. The facts may include any of the following:

(1) Statistical or market indices, market prices of any security or group of securities, interest rates, currency exchange rates, or similar economic or financial data.

(2) A determination or action by the converting domestic corporation or by any other person, group, or body.

(3) The terms of, or actions taken under, an agreement to which the converting domestic corporation is a party, or any other agreement or document.

(b) The following requirements shall be met for a plan of conversion to be approved:

(1) The board of directors shall recommend to the shareholders that the plan of conversion be approved, unless one of the following circumstances exist, in which event the board of directors shall communicate the basis for not recommending approval of the plan of conversion to the shareholders at the time it submits the plan of conversion to the shareholders:

a. The board of directors determines that, because of conflict of interest or other special circumstances, it should not make a recommendation that the shareholders approve the plan of conversion.

b. G.S. 55-8-26 applies.

(2) The shareholders entitled to vote shall approve the plan of conversion.

(c) The board of directors may condition its submission of the proposed conversion on any basis.

(d) The corporation shall notify each shareholder, whether or not entitled to vote, of the proposed shareholders' meeting in accordance with G.S. 55-7-05. The notice shall state that the purpose, or one of the purposes, of the meeting is to consider the plan of conversion and contain or be accompanied by a copy of the plan.

(e) Unless this Chapter, the articles of incorporation, a bylaw adopted by the shareholders or the board of directors, acting pursuant to subsection (c) of this section, require a greater vote or a vote by voting groups, the plan of conversion to be authorized shall be approved by each voting group entitled to vote separately on the plan by a majority of all the votes entitled to be cast on the plan by that voting group and, for the purpose of Article 9 of this Chapter or any provision in the articles of incorporation or bylaws adopted prior to January 1, 2002, a conversion shall be deemed to be included within the term "merger". If any shareholder of the converting domestic corporation has or will have personal liability for any existing or future obligation of the resulting business entity solely as a result of holding an interest in the resulting business entity, then in addition to the requirements of the preceding sentence, approval of the plan of conversion by the domestic corporation shall require the affirmative vote or written consent of that shareholder.

(f) Separate voting by voting groups is required on a plan of conversion if the plan contains a provision that, if contained in a proposed amendment to articles of incorporation, would require action by one or more separate voting groups on the proposed amendment under G.S. 55-10-04, except where the consideration to be received in exchange for the shares of that group consists solely of cash.

(g) After a plan of conversion has been approved by a domestic corporation but before the articles of conversion become effective, the plan of conversion (i) may be amended as provided in the plan of conversion, or (ii) may be abandoned, subject to any contractual rights, as provided in the plan of conversion or, if there is no such provision, as determined by the board of directors without further shareholder action. (2001-387, s. 17; 2005-268, s. 30; 2013-153, s. 11.)

§ 55-11A-12. Articles of conversion.

(a) After a plan of conversion has been approved by the converting domestic corporation as provided in G.S. 55-11A-11, the converting domestic corporation shall deliver articles of conversion to the Secretary of State for filing. The articles of conversion shall state:

(1) The name of the converting domestic corporation;

(2) The name of the resulting business entity, its type of business entity, the state or country whose laws govern its organization and internal affairs, and, if the resulting business entity is not authorized to transact business or conduct affairs in this State, a designation of its mailing address and a commitment to

file with the Secretary of State a statement of any subsequent change in its mailing address; and

(3)   That a plan of conversion has been approved by the domestic corporation as required by law.

(b)   If the domestic corporation is converting to a business entity whose formation, or whose status as a registered limited liability partnership as defined in G.S. 59-32, requires the filing of a document with the Secretary of State, then notwithstanding subsection (a) of this section, the articles of conversion shall be included as part of that document and shall contain the information required by the laws governing the organization and internal affairs of the resulting business entity.

(c)   If the plan of conversion is abandoned after the articles of conversion have been filed with the Secretary of State but before the articles of conversion become effective, the converting domestic corporation shall deliver to the Secretary of State for filing prior to the time the articles of conversion become effective an amendment to the articles of conversion withdrawing the articles of conversion.

(d)   The conversion takes effect when the articles of conversion become effective.

(e)   Certificates of conversion shall also be registered as provided in G.S. 47-18.1. (2001-387, s. 17; 2001-487, s. 62(d).)

§ 55-11A-13. Effects of conversion.

(a)   When the conversion takes effect:

(1)   The converting domestic corporation ceases its prior form of organization and continues in existence as the resulting business entity;

(2)   The title to all real estate and other property owned by the converting domestic corporation continues vested in the resulting business entity without reversion or impairment;

(3) All liabilities of the converting domestic corporation continue as liabilities of the resulting business entity;

(4) A proceeding pending by or against the converting domestic corporation may be continued as if the conversion did not occur;

(5) The shares in the converting domestic corporation that are to be converted into interests, obligations, or securities of the resulting business entity or into the right to receive cash or other property are thereupon so converted, and the former shareholders of the converting domestic corporation are entitled only to the rights provided in the plan of conversion or any rights they may have under Article 13 of this Chapter; and

(6) The resulting business entity is deemed to agree that it will promptly pay to the former shareholders of the converting domestic corporation exercising appraisal rights the amount, if any, to which they are entitled under Article 13 of this Chapter and otherwise to comply with the requirements of Article 13 as if it were a domestic corporation.

The conversion shall not affect the liability or absence of liability of any shareholder of the converting domestic corporation for any acts, omissions, or obligations of the converting domestic corporation made or incurred prior to the effectiveness of the conversion. The cessation of the existence of the converting domestic corporation in its form of organization as a domestic corporation in the conversion shall not constitute a dissolution or termination of the converting domestic corporation.

(b) If the resulting business entity is not a domestic limited liability company or a domestic limited partnership, when the conversion takes effect the resulting business entity is deemed:

(1) To agree that it may be served with process in this State for enforcement of (i) any obligation of the converting domestic corporation, (ii) the appraisal rights of shareholders of the converting domestic corporation under Article 13 of this Chapter, and (iii) any obligation of the resulting business entity arising from the conversion; and

(2) To have appointed the Secretary of State as its agent for service of process in any proceeding described in subdivision (1) of this subsection. Service on the Secretary of State of any such process shall be made by delivering to and leaving with the Secretary of State, or with any clerk authorized

by the Secretary of State to accept service of process, duplicate copies of the process and the fee required by G.S. 55-1-22(b). Upon receipt of service of process on behalf of a resulting business entity in the manner provided for in this section, the Secretary of State shall immediately mail a copy of the process by registered or certified mail, return receipt requested, to the resulting business entity. If the resulting business entity is authorized to transact business or conduct affairs in this State, the address for mailing shall be its principal office designated in the latest document filed with the Secretary of State that is authorized by law to designate the principal office or, if there is no principal office on file, its registered office. If the resulting business entity is not authorized to transact business or conduct affairs in this State, the address for mailing shall be the mailing address designated pursuant to G.S. 55-11A-12(a)(2). (2001-387, s. 17; 2011-347, ss. 10, 11.)

Article 12.

Transfer of Assets.

§ 55-12-01. Disposition of assets not requiring shareholder approval and mortgage of assets.

(a) A mortgage of or other security interest in all or any part of the property of a corporation may be made by authority of the board of directors without approval of the shareholders, unless otherwise provided in the articles of incorporation or in bylaws adopted by the shareholders.

(b) Unless otherwise provided in the articles of incorporation or in bylaws adopted by the shareholders, a corporation may, on the terms and conditions and for the consideration determined by the board of directors, and without approval by the shareholders, do any of the following:

(1) Sell, lease, exchange, or otherwise dispose of all, or substantially all, of its property in the usual and regular course of business.

(2) Transfer any or all of its property to a corporation or an unincorporated entity all the shares or ownership interests of which are owned by the corporation.

(3) Sell, lease, exchange, or otherwise dispose of any of its property, not in the usual and regular course of business, if the sale, lease, exchange, or other disposition is of less than all, or substantially all, of the corporation's property. If the sale, lease, exchange, or other disposition would leave the corporation with a continuing business activity that represented at least twenty-five percent (25%) of total assets at the end of the most recently completed fiscal year and at least twenty-five percent (25%) of either (i) income from continuing operations before taxes or (ii) revenues from continuing operations for that fiscal year, in each case of the corporation and its subsidiaries on a consolidated basis, the sale, lease, exchange, or other disposition will conclusively be deemed to be of less than all, or substantially all, of the corporation's property. (1925, c. 235; 1929, c. 269; 1939, c. 279; G.S., s. 55-26; 1955, c. 1371, s. 1; 1989, c. 265, s. 1; 2001-508, s. 1; 2013-153, s. 12.)

§ 55-12-02. Disposition of assets requiring shareholder approval.

(a) A corporation may sell, lease, exchange, or otherwise dispose of all, or substantially all, of its property, otherwise than in the usual and regular course of business, on the terms and conditions and for the consideration determined by the corporation's board of directors, if the board of directors proposes and its shareholders approve the proposed transaction.

(b) The following requirements shall be met for a transaction to be authorized:

(1) The board of directors shall recommend to the shareholders that the proposed transaction be approved unless one of the following circumstances exist, in which event the board of directors shall communicate the basis for not recommending approval of the proposed transaction to the shareholders at the time it submits the proposed transaction to the shareholders:

a. The board of directors determines that, because of conflict of interest or other special circumstances, it should not make a recommendation that the shareholders approve the proposed transaction.

b. G.S. 55-8-26 applies.

(2) The shareholders entitled to vote must approve the proposed transaction.

(c) The board of directors may condition its submission of the proposed transaction on any basis.

(d) The corporation shall notify each shareholder, whether or not entitled to vote, of the proposed shareholders' meeting in accordance with G.S. 55-7-05. The notice must also state that the purpose, or one of the purposes, of the meeting is to consider the sale, lease, exchange, or other disposition of all, or substantially all, the property of the corporation and contain or be accompanied by a description of the transaction.

(e) Unless the articles of incorporation, a bylaw adopted by the shareholders, Article 9 or the board of directors (acting pursuant to subsection (c)) require a greater vote or a vote by voting groups, the transaction to be authorized must be approved by a majority of all the votes entitled to be cast on the transaction.

(f) After a sale, lease, exchange, or other disposition of property is authorized, the transaction may be abandoned (subject to any contractual rights) without further shareholder action.

(g) A transaction that constitutes a distribution is governed by G.S. 55-6-40 and not by this section. (1925, c. 235; 1929, c. 269; 1939, c. 279; G.S., s. 55-26; 1955, c. 1371, s. 1; 1989, c. 265, s. 1; 2013-153, s. 13.)

§ 55-12-03. Article 9 to control.

Nothing in this Article shall be construed to modify in any manner the provisions or applicability of Article 9. (1989, c. 265, s. 1.)

Article 13.

Appraisal Rights.

Part 1. Right to Appraisal and Payment for Shares.

§ 55-13-01. Definitions.

In this Article, the following definitions apply:

(1) Affiliate. - A person that directly, or indirectly, through one or more intermediaries, controls, is controlled by, or is under common control with another person or is a senior executive thereof. For purposes of G.S. 55-13-01(7), a person is deemed to be an affiliate of its senior executives.

(2) Beneficial shareholder. - A person who is the beneficial owner of shares held in a voting trust or by a nominee on the beneficial owner's behalf.

(3) Corporation. - The issuer of the shares held by a shareholder demanding appraisal and, for matters covered in G.S. 55-13-22 through G.S. 55-13-31, the term includes the surviving entity in a merger.

(4) Expenses. - Reasonable expenses of every kind that are incurred in connection with a matter, including counsel fees.

(5) Fair value. - The value of the corporation's shares (i) immediately before the effectuation of the corporate action as to which the shareholder asserts appraisal rights, excluding any appreciation or depreciation in anticipation of the corporate action unless exclusion would be inequitable, (ii) using customary and current valuation concepts and techniques generally employed for similar business in the context of the transaction requiring appraisal, and (iii) without discounting for lack of marketability or minority status except, if appropriate, for amendments to the articles pursuant to G.S. 55-13-02(a)(5).

(6) Interest. - Interest from the effective date of the corporate action until the date of payment, at the rate of interest on judgments in this State on the effective date of the corporate action.

(7) Interested transaction. - A corporate action described in G.S. 55-13-02(a), other than a merger pursuant to G.S. 55-11-04, involving an interested person and in which any of the shares or assets of the corporation are being acquired or converted. As used in this definition, the following definitions apply:

a. Interested person. - A person, or an affiliate of a person, who at any time during the one-year period immediately preceding approval by the board of directors of the corporate action met any of the following conditions:

1. Was the beneficial owner of twenty percent (20%) or more of the voting power of the corporation, other than as owner of excluded shares.

2. Had the power, contractually or otherwise, other than as owner of excluded shares, to cause the appointment or election of twenty-five percent (25%) or more of the directors to the board of directors of the corporation.

3. Was a senior executive or director of the corporation or a senior executive of any affiliate thereof, and that senior executive or director will receive, as a result of the corporate action, a financial benefit not generally available to other shareholders as such, other than any of the following:

I. Employment, consulting, retirement, or similar benefits established separately and not as part of or in contemplation of the corporate action.

II. Employment, consulting, retirement, or similar benefits established in contemplation of, or as part of, the corporate action that are not more favorable than those existing before the corporate action or, if more favorable, that have been approved on behalf of the corporation in the same manner as is provided in G.S. 55-8-31(a)(1) and (c).

III. In the case of a director of the corporation who will, in the corporate action, become a director of the acquiring entity, or one of its affiliates, rights and benefits as a director that are provided on the same basis as those afforded by the acquiring entity generally to other directors of the acquiring entity or such affiliate of the acquiring entity.

b. Beneficial owner. - Any person who, directly or indirectly, through any contract, arrangement, or understanding, other than a revocable proxy, has or shares the power to vote, or to direct the voting of, shares. If a member of a national securities exchange is precluded by the rules of the exchange from voting without instruction on contested matters or matters that may affect substantially the rights or privileges of the holders of the securities to be voted, then that member of a national securities exchange shall not be deemed a "beneficial owner" of any securities held directly or indirectly by the member on behalf of another person solely because the member is the record holder of the securities. When two or more persons agree to act together for the purpose of voting their shares of the corporation, each member of the group formed thereby is deemed to have acquired beneficial ownership, as of the date of the agreement, of all voting shares of the corporation beneficially owned by any member of the group.

c. Excluded shares. - Shares acquired pursuant to an offer for all shares having voting power if the offer was made within one year prior to the corporate action for consideration of the same kind and of a value equal to or less than that paid in connection with the corporate action.

(8) Preferred shares. - A class or series of shares the holders of which have preference over any other class or series with respect to distributions.

(9) Record shareholder. - The person in whose name shares are registered in the records of the corporation or the beneficial owner of shares to the extent of the rights granted by a nominee certificate on file with the corporation.

(10) Senior executive. - The chief executive officer, chief operating officer, chief financial officer, or anyone in charge of a principal business unit or function.

(11) Shareholder. - Both a record shareholder and a beneficial shareholder. (1925, c. 77, s. 1; 1943, c. 270; G.S., s. 55-167; 1955, c. 1371, s. 1; 1969, c. 751, s. 39; 1973, c. 469, ss. 36, 37; 1989, c. 265, s. 1; 2011-347, s. 1.)

§ 55-13-02. Right to appraisal.

(a) In addition to any rights granted under Article 9, a shareholder is entitled to appraisal rights and to obtain payment of the fair value of that shareholder's shares, in the event of any of the following corporate actions:

(1) Consummation of a merger to which the corporation is a party if either (i) shareholder approval is required for the merger by G.S. 55-11-03 and the shareholder is entitled to vote on the merger, except that appraisal rights shall not be available to any shareholder of the corporation with respect to shares of any class or series that remain outstanding after consummation of the merger or (ii) the corporation is a subsidiary and the merger is governed by G.S. 55-11-04.

(2) Consummation of a share exchange to which the corporation is a party as the corporation whose shares will be acquired if the shareholder is entitled to vote on the exchange, except that appraisal rights shall not be available to any shareholder of the corporation with respect to any class or series of shares of the corporation that is not exchanged.

(3) Consummation of a disposition of assets pursuant to G.S. 55-12-02 if the shareholder is entitled to vote on the disposition.

(4) An amendment of the articles of incorporation (i) with respect to a class or series of shares that reduces the number of shares of a class or series owned by the shareholder to a fraction of a share if the corporation has an obligation or right to repurchase the fractional share so created or (ii) changes the corporation into a nonprofit corporation or cooperative organization.

(5) Any other amendment to the articles of incorporation, merger, share exchange, or disposition of assets to the extent provided by the articles of incorporation, bylaws, or a resolution of the board of directors.

(6) Consummation of a conversion to a foreign corporation pursuant to Part 2 of Article 11A of this Chapter if the shareholder does not receive shares in the foreign corporation resulting from the conversion that (i) have terms as favorable to the shareholder in all material respects and (ii) represent at least the same percentage interest of the total voting rights of the outstanding shares of the corporation as the shares held by the shareholder before the conversion.

(7) Consummation of a conversion of the corporation to nonprofit status pursuant to Part 2 of Article 11A of this Chapter.

(8) Consummation of a conversion of the corporation to an unincorporated entity pursuant to Part 2 of Article 11A of this Chapter.

(b) Notwithstanding subsection (a) of this section, the availability of appraisal rights under subdivisions (1), (2), (3), (4), (6), and (8) of subsection (a) of this section shall be limited in accordance with the following provisions:

(1) Appraisal rights shall not be available for the holders of shares of any class or series of shares that are any of the following:

a. A covered security under section 18(b)(1)(A) or (B) of the Securities Act of 1933, as amended.

b. Traded in an organized market and has at least 2,000 shareholders and a market value of at least twenty million dollars ($20,000,000)(exclusive of the value of shares held by the corporation's subsidiaries, senior executives, directors, and beneficial shareholders owning more than ten percent (10%) of such shares).

c. Issued by an open-end management investment company registered with the Securities and Exchange Commission under the Investment Company Act of 1940, as amended, and may be redeemed at the option of the holder at net asset value.

(2) The applicability of subdivision (1) of this subsection shall be determined as of (i) the record date fixed to determine the shareholders entitled to receive notice of, and to vote at, the meeting of shareholders to act upon the corporate action requiring appraisal rights or (ii) the day before the effective date of such corporate action if there is no meeting of shareholders.

(3) Subdivision (1) of this subsection shall not be applicable and appraisal rights shall be available pursuant to subsection (a) of this section for the holders of any class or series of shares who are required by the terms of the corporate action requiring appraisal rights to accept for such shares anything other than cash or shares of any class or any series of shares of any corporation, or any other proprietary interest of any other entity, that satisfies the standards set forth in subdivision (1) of this subsection at the time the corporate action becomes effective.

(4) Subdivision (1) of this subsection shall not be applicable and appraisal rights shall be available pursuant to subsection (a) of this section for the holders of any class or series of shares where the corporate action is an interested transaction.

(c) Notwithstanding any other provision of this section, the articles of incorporation as originally filed or any amendment to the articles may limit or eliminate appraisal rights for any class or series of preferred shares. Any amendment to the articles that limits or eliminates appraisal rights for any shares that are outstanding immediately prior to the effective date of the amendment or that the corporation is or may be required to issue or sell thereafter pursuant to any conversion, exchange, or other right existing immediately before the effective date of the amendment, however, shall not apply to any corporate action that becomes effective within one year of that date if the corporate action would otherwise afford appraisal rights.

(d) A shareholder holding shares of a class or series that were issued and outstanding as of the effective date of this act but that did not as of that date entitle the shareholder to vote on a corporate action described in subdivision (a)(1), (2), or (3) of this section shall be entitled to appraisal rights, and to obtain payment of the fair value of the shareholder's shares of such class or series, to the same extent as if such shares did entitle the shareholder to vote on such corporate action. (1925, c. 77, s. 1; c. 235; 1929, c. 269; 1939, c. 279; 1943, c. 270; G.S., ss. 55-26, 55-167; 1955, c. 1371, s. 1; 1959, c. 1316, ss. 30, 31; 1969, c. 751, ss. 36, 39; 1973, c. 469, ss. 36, 37; c. 476, s. 193; 1989, c. 265, s. 1; 1989 (Reg. Sess., 1990), c. 1024, s. 12.18; 1991, c. 645, s. 12; 1997-202, s. 1; 1999-141, s. 1; 2001-387, s. 26; 2003-157, s. 1; 2011-347, ss. 1, 22(c).)

§ 55-13-03. Assertion of rights by nominees and beneficial owners.

(a) A record shareholder may assert appraisal rights as to fewer than all the shares registered in the record shareholder's name but owned by a beneficial shareholder only if the record shareholder (i) objects with respect to all shares of the class or series owned by the beneficial shareholder and (ii) notifies the corporation in writing of the name and address of each beneficial shareholder on whose behalf appraisal rights are being asserted. The rights of a record shareholder who asserts appraisal rights for only part of the shares held of record in the record shareholder's name under this subsection shall be determined as if the shares as to which the record shareholder objects and the record shareholder's other shares were registered in the names of different record shareholders.

(b) A beneficial shareholder may assert appraisal rights as to shares of any class or series held on behalf of the shareholder only if the shareholder does both of the following:

(1) Submits to the corporation the record shareholder's written consent to the assertion of rights no later than the date referred to in G.S. 55-13-22(b)(2)b.

(2) Submits written consent under subdivision (1) of this subsection with respect to all shares of the class or series that are beneficially owned by the beneficial shareholder. (1925, c. 77, s. 1; 1943, c. 270; G.S., s. 55-167; 1955, c.

1371, s. 1; 1969, c. 751, s. 39; 1973, c. 469, ss. 36, 37; 1989, c. 265, s. 1; 2011-347, s. 1.)

§§ 55-13-04 through 55-13-19. Reserved for future codification purposes.

Part 2. Procedure for Exercise of Appraisal Rights.

§ 55-13-20. Notice of appraisal rights.

(a)   If any corporate action specified in G.S. 55-13-02(a) is to be submitted to a vote at a shareholders' meeting, the meeting notice must state that the corporation has concluded that shareholders are, are not, or may be entitled to assert appraisal rights under this Article. If the corporation concludes that appraisal rights are or may be available, a copy of this Article must accompany the meeting notice sent to those record shareholders entitled to exercise appraisal rights.

(b)   In a merger pursuant to G.S. 55-11-04, the parent corporation must notify in writing all record shareholders of the subsidiary who are entitled to assert appraisal rights that the corporate action became effective. In the case of any other corporate action specified in G.S. 55-13-02(a) with respect to which shareholders of a class or series do not have the right to vote, but with respect to which those shareholders are entitled to assert appraisal rights, the corporation must notify in writing all record shareholders of such class or series that the corporate action became effective. Notice required under this subsection must be sent within 10 days after the corporate action became effective and include the materials described in G.S. 55-13-22.

(c)   If any corporate action specified in G.S. 55-13-02(a) is to be approved by written consent of the shareholders pursuant to G.S. 55-7-04, then the following must occur:

(1)   Written notice that appraisal rights are, are not, or may be available must be given to each record shareholder from whom a consent is solicited at the time consent of each shareholder is first solicited and, if the corporation has concluded that appraisal rights are or may be available, must be accompanied by a copy of this Article.

158

(2) Written notice that appraisal rights are, are not, or may be available must be delivered together with the notice to the applicable shareholders required by subsections (d) and (e) of G.S. 55-7-04, may include the materials described in G.S. 55-13-22, and, if the corporation has concluded that appraisal rights are or may be available, must be accompanied by a copy of this Article.

(d) If any corporate action described in G.S. 55-13-02(a) is proposed, or a merger pursuant to G.S. 55-11-04 is effected, then the notice referred to in subsection (a) or (c) of this section, if the corporation concludes that appraisal rights are or may be available, and in subsection (b) of this section shall be accompanied by the following:

(1) The annual financial statements specified in G.S. 55-16-20(a) of the corporation that issued the shares to be appraised. The date of the financial statements shall not be more than 16 months before the date of the notice and shall comply with G.S. 55-16-20(b). If annual financial statements that meet the requirements of this subdivision are not reasonably available, then the corporation shall provide reasonably equivalent financial information.

(2) The latest available quarterly financial statements of the corporation, if any.

The right to receive the information described in this subsection may be waived in writing by a shareholder before or after the corporate action. (1925, c. 77, s. 1; c. 235; 1929, c. 269; 1939, c. 5; c. 279; 1943, c. 270; G.S., ss. 55-26, 55-165, 55-167; 1955, c. 1371, s. 1; 1969, c. 751, s. 39; 1973, c. 469, ss. 36, 37; 1989, c. 265, s. 1; 2002-58, s. 2; 2011-347, s. 1.)

§ 55-13-21. Notice of intent to demand payment and consequences of voting or consenting.

(a) If a corporate action specified in G.S. 55-13-02(a) is submitted to a vote at a shareholders' meeting, a shareholder who is entitled to vote on the corporate action and who wishes to assert appraisal rights with respect to any class or series of shares must do the following:

(1) Deliver to the corporation, before the vote is taken, written notice of the shareholder's intent to demand payment if the proposed action is effectuated.

(2) Not vote, or cause or permit to be voted, any shares of any class or series in favor of the proposed action.

(b) If a corporate action specified in G.S. 55-13-02(a) is to be approved by less than unanimous written consent, a shareholder who is entitled to vote on the corporate action and who wishes to assert appraisal rights with respect to any class or series of shares must not execute a consent in favor of the proposed action with respect to that class or series of shares.

(c) A shareholder who fails to satisfy the requirements of subsection (a) or (b) of this section is not entitled to payment under this Article. (1925, c. 77, s. 1; 1943, c. 270; G.S., s. 55-167; 1955, c. 1371, s. 1; 1969, c. 751, s. 39; 1973, c. 469, ss. 36, 37; 1989, c. 265, s. 1; 2011-347, s. 1.)

§ 55-13-22. Appraisal notice and form.

(a) If a corporate action requiring appraisal rights under G.S. 55-13-02(a) becomes effective, the corporation must deliver a written appraisal notice and form required by subdivision (b)(1) of this section to all shareholders who satisfied the requirements of G.S. 55-13-21. In the case of a merger under G.S. 55-11-04, the parent corporation must deliver a written appraisal notice and form to all record shareholders of the subsidiary who may be entitled to assert appraisal rights. In the case of any other corporate action specified in G.S. 55-13-02(a) that becomes effective and with respect to which shareholders of a class or series do not have the right to vote but with respect to which such shareholders are entitled to assert appraisal rights, the corporation must deliver a written appraisal notice and form to all record shareholders of such class or series who may be entitled to assert appraisal rights.

(b) The appraisal notice must be sent no earlier than the date the corporate action specified in G.S. 55-13-02(a) became effective and no later than 10 days after that date. The appraisal notice must include the following:

(1) A form that specifies the first date of any announcement to shareholders, made prior to the date the corporate action became effective, of the principal terms of the proposed corporate action. If such an announcement was made, the form shall require a shareholder asserting appraisal rights to certify whether beneficial ownership of those shares for which appraisal rights

are asserted was acquired before that date. The form shall require a shareholder asserting appraisal rights to certify that the shareholder did not vote for or consent to the transaction.

(2) Disclosure of the following:

a. Where the form must be sent and where certificates for certificated shares must be deposited, as well as the date by which those certificates must be deposited. The certificate deposit date must not be earlier than the date for receiving the required form under sub-subdivision b. of this subdivision.

b. A date by which the corporation must receive the payment demand, which date may not be fewer than 40 nor more than 60 days after the date the appraisal notice required under subsection (a) of this section and form are sent. The form shall also state that the shareholder shall have waived the right to demand appraisal with respect to the shares unless the form is received by the corporation by the specified date.

c. The corporation's estimate of the fair value of the shares.

d. That, if requested in writing, the corporation will provide, to the shareholder so requesting, within 10 days after the date specified in sub-subdivision b. of this subdivision, the number of shareholders who return the forms by the specified date and the total number of shares owned by them.

e. The date by which the notice to withdraw under G.S. 55-13-23 must be received, which date must be within 20 days after the date specified in sub-subdivision b. of this subdivision.

(3) Be accompanied by a copy of this Article. (1925, c. 77, s. 1; 1943, c. 270; G.S., s. 55-167; 1955, c. 1371, s. 1; 1969, c. 751, s. 39; 1973, c. 469, ss. 36, 37; 1989, c. 265, s. 1; 1997-485, s. 4; 2001-387, s. 27; 2002-58, s. 3; 2011-347, s. 1.)

§ 55-13-23. Perfection of rights; right to withdraw.

(a) A shareholder who receives notice pursuant to G.S. 55-13-22 and who wishes to exercise appraisal rights must sign and return the form sent by the corporation and, in the case of certificated shares, deposit the shareholder's certificates in accordance with the terms of the notice by the date referred to in the notice pursuant to G.S. 55-13-22(b)(2). In addition, if applicable, the shareholder must certify on the form whether the beneficial owner of such shares acquired beneficial ownership of the shares before the date required to be set forth in the notice pursuant to G.S. 55-13-22(b)(1). If a shareholder fails to make this certification, the corporation may elect to treat the shareholder's shares as after-acquired shares under G.S. 55-13-27. Once a shareholder deposits that shareholder's certificates or, in the case of uncertificated shares, returns the signed forms, that shareholder loses all rights as a shareholder, unless the shareholder withdraws pursuant to subsection (b) of this section.

(b) A shareholder who has complied with subsection (a) of this section may nevertheless decline to exercise appraisal rights and withdraw from the appraisal process by so notifying the corporation in writing by the date set forth in the appraisal notice pursuant to G.S. 55-13-22(b)(2)e. A shareholder who fails to so withdraw from the appraisal process may not thereafter withdraw without the corporation's written consent.

(c) A shareholder who does not sign and return the form and, in the case of certificated shares, deposit that shareholder's share certificates where required, each by the date set forth in the notice described in G.S. 55-13-22(b) shall not be entitled to payment under this Article. (1925, c. 77, s. 1; 1943, c. 270; G.S., s. 55-167; 1955, c. 1371, s. 1; 1969, c. 751, s. 39; 1973, c. 469, ss. 36, 37; 1989, c. 265, s. 1; 2011-347, s. 1.)

§ 55-13-24: Repealed by Session Laws 2011-347, s. 1, effective October 1, 2011.

§ 55-13-25. Payment.

(a) Except as provided in G.S. 55-13-27, within 30 days after the form required by G.S. 55-13-22(b) is due, the corporation shall pay in cash to the shareholders who complied with G.S. 55-13-23(a) the amount the corporation estimates to be the fair value of their shares, plus interest.

(b) The payment to each shareholder pursuant to subsection (a) of this section must be accompanied by the following:

(1) The following financial information:

a. The annual financial statements specified in G.S. 55-16-20(a) of the corporation that issued the shares to be appraised. The date of the financial statements shall not be more than 16 months before the date of payment and shall comply with G.S. 55-16-20(b). If annual financial statements that meet the requirements of this sub-subdivision are not reasonably available, the corporation shall provide reasonably equivalent financial information.

b. The latest available quarterly financial statements, if any.

(2) A statement of the corporation's estimate of the fair value of the shares. The estimate must equal or exceed the corporation's estimate given pursuant to G.S. 55-13-22(b)(2)c.

(3) A statement that the shareholders described in subsection (a) of this section have the right to demand further payment under G.S. 55-13-28 and that if a shareholder does not do so within the time period specified therein, then the shareholder shall be deemed to have accepted such payment in full satisfaction of the corporation's obligations under this Article. (1925, c. 77, s. 1; 1943, c. 270; G.S., s. 55-167; 1955, c. 1371, s. 1; 1969, c. 751, s. 39; 1973, c. 469, ss. 36, 37; 1989, c. 265, s. 1; c. 770, s. 69; 1997-202, s. 2; 2011-347, s. 1.)

§ 55-13-26: Repealed by Session Laws 2011-347, s. 1, effective October 1, 2011.

§ 55-13-27. After-acquired shares.

(a) A corporation may elect to withhold payment required by G.S. 55-13-25 from any shareholder who was required to but did not certify that beneficial ownership of all of the shareholder's shares for which appraisal rights are asserted was acquired before the date set forth in the appraisal notice sent pursuant to G.S. 55-13-22(b)(1).

(b) If the corporation elected to withhold payment under subsection (a) of this section, it must, within 30 days after the form required by G.S. 55-13-22(b) is due, notify all shareholders who are described in subsection (a) of this section of the following:

(1)   The information required by G.S. 55-13-25(b)(1).

(2)   The corporation's estimate of fair value pursuant to G.S. 55-13-25(b)(2).

(3)   That they may accept the corporation's estimate of fair value, plus interest, in full satisfaction of their demands or demand appraisal under G.S. 55-13-28.

(4)   That those shareholders who wish to accept such offer must so notify the corporation of their acceptance of the corporation's offer within 30 days after receiving the offer.

(5)   That those shareholders who do not satisfy the requirements for demanding appraisal under G.S. 55-13-28 shall be deemed to have accepted the corporation's offer.

(c)   Within 10 days after receiving the shareholder's acceptance pursuant to subsection (b) of this section, the corporation must pay in cash the amount it offered under subdivision (b)(2) of this section to each shareholder who agreed to accept the corporation's offer in full satisfaction of the shareholder's demand.

(d)   Within 40 days after sending the notice described in subsection (b) of this section, the corporation must pay in cash the amount it offered to pay under subdivision (b)(2) of this section to each shareholder described in subdivision (b)(5) of this section. (2011-347, s. 1.)

§ 55-13-28. Procedure if shareholder dissatisfied with payment or offer.

(a)   A shareholder paid pursuant to G.S. 55-13-25 who is dissatisfied with the amount of the payment must notify the corporation in writing of that shareholder's estimate of the fair value of the shares and demand payment of that estimate plus interest (less any payment under G.S. 55-13-25). A shareholder offered payment under G.S. 55-13-27 who is dissatisfied with that offer must reject the offer and demand payment of the shareholder's stated estimate of the fair value of the shares, plus interest.

(b) A shareholder who fails to notify the corporation in writing of that shareholder's demand to be paid the shareholder's stated estimate of the fair value, plus interest, under subsection (a) of this section within 30 days after receiving the corporation's payment or offer of payment under G.S. 55-13-25 or G.S. 55-13-27, respectively, waives the right to demand payment under this section and shall be entitled only to the payment made or offered pursuant to those respective sections. (1925, c. 77, s. 1; 1943, c. 270; G.S., s. 55-167; 1955, c. 1371, s. 1; 1969, c. 751, s. 39; 1973, c. 469, ss. 36, 37; 1989, c. 265, s. 1; 1997-202, s. 3; 2011-347, s. 1.)

§ 55-13-29. Reserved for future codification purposes.

Part 3. Judicial Appraisal of Shares.

§ 55-13-30. Court Action.

(a) If a shareholder makes a demand for payment under G.S. 55-13-28 which remains unsettled, the corporation shall commence a proceeding within 60 days after receiving the payment demand by filing a complaint with the Superior Court Division of the General Court of Justice to determine the fair value of the shares and accrued interest. If the corporation does not commence the proceeding within the 60-day period, the corporation shall pay in cash to each shareholder the amount the shareholder demanded pursuant to G.S. 55-13-28, plus interest.

(a1) Repealed by Session Laws 1997-202, s. 4.

(b) The corporation shall commence the proceeding in the appropriate court of the county where the corporation's principal office (or, if none, its registered office) in this State is located. If the corporation is a foreign corporation without a registered office in this State, it shall commence the proceeding in the county in this State where the principal office or registered office of the domestic corporation merged with the foreign corporation was located at the time of the transaction.

(c) The corporation shall make all shareholders (whether or not residents of this State) whose demands remain unsettled parties to the proceeding as in an action against their shares and all parties must be served with a copy of the complaint. Nonresidents may be served by registered or certified mail or by publication as provided by law.

(d) The jurisdiction of the superior court in which the proceeding is commenced under subsection (b) of this section is plenary and exclusive. The court may appoint one or more persons as appraisers to receive evidence and recommend a decision on the question of fair value. The appraisers shall have the powers described in the order appointing them, or in any amendment to it. The shareholders demanding appraisal rights are entitled to the same discovery rights as parties in other civil proceedings. There shall be no right to a trial by jury.

(e) Each shareholder made a party to the proceeding is entitled to judgment either (i) for the amount, if any, by which the court finds the fair value of the shareholder's shares, plus interest, exceeds the amount paid by the corporation to the shareholder for the shareholder's shares or (ii) for the fair value, plus interest, of the shareholder's shares for which the corporation elected to withhold payment under G.S. 55-13-27. (1925, c. 77, s. 1; 1943, c. 270; G.S., s. 55-167; 1955, c. 1371, s. 1; 1969, c. 751, s. 39; 1973, c. 469, ss. 36, 37; 1989, c. 265, s. 1; 1997-202, s. 4; 1997-485, ss. 5, 5.1; 2011-347, s. 1.)

§ 55-13-31. Court costs and expenses.

(a) The court in an appraisal proceeding commenced under G.S. 55-13-30 shall determine all court costs of the proceeding, including the reasonable compensation and expenses of appraisers appointed by the court. The court shall assess the costs against the corporation, except that the court may assess costs against all or some of the shareholders demanding appraisal, in amounts the court finds equitable, to the extent the court finds such shareholders acted arbitrarily, vexatiously, or not in good faith with respect to the rights provided by this Article.

(b) The court in an appraisal proceeding may also assess the expenses for the respective parties, in amounts the court finds equitable:

(1) Against the corporation and in favor of any or all shareholders demanding appraisal if the court finds the corporation did not substantially

comply with the requirements of G.S. 55-13-20, 55-13-22, 55-13-25, or 55-13-27.

(2) Against either the corporation or a shareholder demanding appraisal, in favor of any other party, if the court finds that the party against whom expenses are assessed acted arbitrarily, vexatiously, or not in good faith with respect to the rights provided by this Article.

(c) If the court in an appraisal proceeding finds that the expenses incurred by any shareholder were of substantial benefit to other shareholders similarly situated and that these expenses should not be assessed against the corporation, the court may direct that the expenses be paid out of the amounts awarded the shareholders who were benefited.

(d) To the extent the corporation fails to make a required payment pursuant to G.S. 55-13-25, 55-13-27, or 55-13-28, the shareholder may sue directly for the amount owed and, to the extent successful, shall be entitled to recover from the corporation all expenses of the suit. (1925, c. 77, s. 1; 1943, c. 270; G.S., s. 55-167; 1955, c. 1371, s. 1; 1969, c. 751, s. 39; 1973, c. 469, ss. 36, 37; 1989, c. 265, s. 1; 2011-347, s. 1.)

§ 55-13-32: Reserved for future codification purposes.

§ 55-13-33: Reserved for future codification purposes.

§ 55-13-34: Reserved for future codification purposes.

§ 55-13-35: Reserved for future codification purposes.

§ 55-13-36: Reserved for future codification purposes.

§ 55-13-37: Reserved for future codification purposes.

§ 55-13-38: Reserved for future codification purposes.

§ 55-13-39: Reserved for future codification purposes.

Part 4. Other Remedies.

§ 55-13-40. Other remedies limited.

(a) The legality of a proposed or completed corporate action described in G.S. 55-13-02(a) may not be contested, nor may the corporate action be enjoined, set aside, or rescinded, in a legal or equitable proceeding by a shareholder after the shareholders have approved the corporate action.

(b) Subsection (a) of this section does not apply to a corporate action that:

(1) Was not authorized and approved in accordance with the applicable provisions of any of the following:

a. Article 9, 9A, 10, 11, 11A, or 12 of this Chapter.

b. The articles of incorporation or bylaws.

c. The resolution of the board of directors authorizing the corporate action.

(2) Was procured as a result of fraud, a material misrepresentation, or an omission of a material fact necessary to make statements made, in light of the circumstances in which they were made, not misleading.

(3) Constitutes an interested transaction, unless it has been authorized, approved, or ratified by either (i) the board of directors or a committee of the board or (ii) the shareholders, in the same manner as is provided in G.S. 55-8-

31(a)(1) and (c) or in G.S. 55-8-31(a)(2) and (d), as if the interested transaction were a director's conflict of interest transaction.

(4) Was approved by less than unanimous consent of the voting shareholders pursuant to G.S. 55-7-04, provided that both of the following are true:

a. The challenge to the corporate action is brought by a shareholder who did not consent and as to whom notice of the approval of the corporate action was not effective at least 10 days before the corporate action was effected.

b. The proceeding challenging the corporate action is commenced within 10 days after notice of the approval of the corporate action is effective as to the shareholder bringing the proceeding. (2011-347, s. 1.)

Article 14.

Dissolution.

Part 1. Voluntary Dissolution.

§ 55-14-01. Dissolution by incorporators or directors.

(a) The board of directors or, if the corporation has no directors, a majority of the incorporators of a corporation that has not issued shares may dissolve the corporation by delivering to the Secretary of State for filing articles of dissolution that set forth:

(1) The name of the corporation;

(1a) The names and addresses of its officers, if any;

(1b) The names and addresses of its directors, if any, or if none, the names and addresses of its incorporators;

(2) The date of its incorporation;

(3) That none of the corporation's shares has been issued;

(4) That no debt of the corporation remains unpaid;

(5) Reserved for future codification purposes; and

(6) That a majority of the incorporators or the board of directors authorized the dissolution.

(b) A corporation is dissolved upon the effective date of its articles of dissolution. (1955, c. 1371, s. 1; 1959, c. 1316, s. 261/2; 1989, c. 265, s. 1; 1989 (Reg. Sess., 1990), c. 1024, s. 12.19.)

§ 55-14-02. Dissolution by board of directors and shareholders.

(a) A corporation's board of directors may propose dissolution for submission to the shareholders.

(b) The following requirements shall be met for a proposal to dissolve to be adopted:

(1) The board of directors shall recommend to the shareholders that the proposal to dissolve be approved unless one of the following circumstances exist, in which event the board of directors shall communicate the basis for not recommending approval of the proposal to dissolve to the shareholders at the time it submits the proposal to dissolve to the shareholders:

a. The board of directors determines that, because of conflict of interest or other special circumstances, it should not make a recommendation that the shareholders approve the proposal to dissolve.

b. G.S. 55-8-26 applies.

(2) The shareholders entitled to vote must approve the proposal to dissolve as provided in subsection (e).

(c) The board of directors may condition its submission of the proposal for dissolution on any basis.

(d) The corporation shall notify each shareholder, whether or not entitled to vote, of the proposed shareholders' meeting in accordance with G.S. 55-7-05.

The notice must also state that the purpose, or one of the purposes, of the meeting is to consider dissolving the corporation.

(e) Unless the articles of incorporation, a bylaw adopted by the shareholders, or the board of directors (acting pursuant to subsection (c)) require a greater vote or a vote by voting groups, the proposal to dissolve to be adopted must be approved by a majority of all the votes entitled to be cast on that proposal. (1901, c. 2, s. 34; Rev., s. 1195; C.S., s. 1182; 1941, c. 195; G.S., s. 55-121; 1951, c. 1005, s. 4; 1955, c. 1371, s. 1; 1989, c. 265, s. 1; 2013-153, s. 14.)

§ 55-14-03. Articles of dissolution.

(a) At any time after dissolution is authorized pursuant to G.S. 55-14-02, the corporation may dissolve by delivering to the Secretary of State for filing articles of dissolution setting forth:

(1) The name of the corporation;

(1a) The names and addresses of its officers;

(1b) The names and addresses of its directors;

(2) The date dissolution was authorized;

(3) A statement that shareholder approval was obtained as required by this Chapter.

(4) Repealed by Session Laws 1991, c. 645, s. 10(c).

(b) A corporation is dissolved upon the effective date of its articles of dissolution.

(c) For purposes of this Chapter, a dissolved corporation is a corporation whose articles of dissolution have become effective and includes a successor entity to which the remaining assets of the corporation are transferred subject to its liabilities for purposes of a liquidation. (1901, c. 2, s. 34; Rev., s. 1195; C.S., s. 1182; 1941, c. 195; G.S., s. 55-121; 1951, c. 1005, s. 4; 1955, c. 1371, s. 1; 1989, c. 265, s. 1; 1991, c. 645, s. 10(c); 2005-268, s. 31.)

§ 55-14-04. Revocation of dissolution.

(a)   A corporation may revoke its dissolution within 120 days after its effective date.

(b)   Revocation of dissolution must be authorized in the same manner as the dissolution was authorized unless an authorization under G.S. 55-14-02 permitted revocation by action of the board of directors alone, in which event the board of directors may revoke the dissolution without shareholder action.

(c)   After the revocation of dissolution is authorized, the corporation may revoke the dissolution by delivering to the Secretary of State for filing articles of revocation of dissolution, together with a copy of its articles of dissolution, that set forth:

(1)   The name of the corporation;

(2)   The effective date of the dissolution that was revoked;

(3)   The date that the revocation of dissolution was authorized;

(4)   If the corporation's board of directors (or incorporators) revoked the dissolution, a statement to that effect;

(5)   If the corporation's board of directors revoked a dissolution authorized by the shareholders, a statement that revocation was permitted by action by the board of directors alone pursuant to that authorization; and

(6)   If shareholder action was required to revoke the dissolution, the information required by G.S. 55-14-03(a)(3) or (4) with respect to the revocation.

(d)   Revocation of dissolution is effective upon the effective date of the articles of revocation of dissolution.

(e)   When the revocation of dissolution is effective, it relates back to and takes effect as of the effective date of the dissolution and the corporation resumes carrying on its business as if dissolution had never occurred, subject to the rights of any person who reasonably relied to his prejudice upon the filing of the articles of dissolution. (1955, c. 1371, s. 1; 1989, c. 265, s. 1.)

§ 55-14-05. Effect of dissolution.

(a) A dissolved corporation continues its corporate existence but may not carry on any business except that appropriate to wind up and liquidate its business and affairs, including:

(1) Collecting its assets;

(2) Disposing of its properties that will not be distributed in kind to its shareholders;

(3) Discharging or making provision for discharging its liabilities;

(4) Distributing its remaining property among its shareholders according to their interests; and

(5) Doing every other act necessary to wind up and liquidate its business and affairs.

(b) Dissolution of a corporation does not:

(1) Transfer title to the corporation's property;

(2) Prevent transfer of its shares or securities, although the authorization to dissolve may provide for closing the corporation's share transfer records;

(3) Subject its directors or officers to standards of conduct different from those prescribed in Article 8;

(4) Change quorum or voting requirements for its board of directors or shareholders; change provisions for selection, resignation, or removal of its directors or officers or both; or change provisions for amending its bylaws;

(5) Prevent commencement of a proceeding by or against the corporation in its corporate name;

(6) Abate or suspend a proceeding pending by or against the corporation on the effective date of dissolution; or

(7) Terminate the authority of the registered agent of the corporation.

(c) After the end of the tax year in which dissolution occurs, a dissolved corporation is not subject to the annual franchise tax unless it engages in business activities not appropriate to winding up and liquidating its business and affairs as permitted by subsection (a). (1955, c. 1371, s. 1; 1973, c. 469, ss. 39, 40, c. 476, s. 193; 1989, c. 265, s. 1.)

§ 55-14-06. Known claims against dissolved corporation.

(a) A dissolved corporation may dispose of the known claims against it by following the procedure described in this section.

(b) The dissolved corporation shall notify its known claimants in writing of the dissolution at any time after its effective date. The written notice must:

(1) Describe information that must be included in a claim;

(2) Provide a mailing address where a claim may be sent;

(3) State the deadline, which may not be fewer than 120 days from the effective date of the written notice, by which the dissolved corporation must receive the claim; and

(4) State that the claim will be barred if not received by the deadline.

(c) A claim against the dissolved corporation is barred:

(1) If the corporation does not receive the claim by the deadline from a claimant who received written notice under subsection (b); or

(2) If a claimant whose claim was rejected by written notice from the dissolved corporation does not commence a proceeding to enforce the claim within 90 days from the date of receipt of the rejection notice.

(d)   For purposes of this section, "claim" does not include a contingent liability or a claim based on an event occurring after the effective date of dissolution. (1955, c. 1371, s. 1; 1973, c. 469, ss. 39, 40, c. 476, s. 193; 1989, c. 265, s. 1.)

§ 55-14-07. Unknown and certain other claims against dissolved corporation.

(a)   A dissolved corporation may also publish notice of its dissolution and request that persons with claims against the corporation present them in accordance with the notice.

(b)   The notice must:

(1)   Be published one time in a newspaper of general circulation in the county where the dissolved corporation's principal office (or, if none in this State, its registered office) is or was last located;

(2)   Describe the information that must be included in a claim and provide a mailing address where the claim may be sent; and

(3)   State that a claim against the corporation will be barred unless a proceeding to enforce the claim is commenced within five years after the publication of the notice.

(c)   If the dissolved corporation publishes a newspaper notice in accordance with subsection (b), the claim of each of the following claimants is barred unless the claimant commences a proceeding to enforce the claim against the dissolved corporation within five years after the publication date of the newspaper notice:

(1)   A claimant who did not receive written notice under G.S. 55-14-06;

(2)   A claimant whose claim was timely sent to the dissolved corporation but not acted on;

(3)   A claimant whose claim is contingent or based on an event occurring after the effective date of dissolution. (1955, c. 1371, s. 1; 1973, c. 469, ss. 39, 40, c. 476, s. 193; 1989, c. 265, s. 1.)

§ 55-14-08. Enforcement of claims.

(a) A claim under G.S. 55-14-06 or G.S. 55-14-07 may be enforced:

(1) Against the dissolved corporation, to the extent of its undistributed assets, including coverage under any applicable insurance policy, or

(2) Except as provided in G.S. 55-14-09(d), if the assets have been distributed in liquidation, against a shareholder of the dissolved corporation to the extent of the shareholder's pro rata share of the claim or the corporate assets distributed to the shareholder in liquidation, whichever is less, but a shareholder's total liability for all claims under this section may not exceed the total amount of assets distributed to the shareholder.

(b) Nothing in G.S. 55-14-06 or G.S. 55-14-07 shall extend any applicable period of limitation. (1955, c. 1371, s. 1; 1973, c. 469, ss. 39, 40; 1989, c. 265, s. 1; 2005-268, s. 32.)

§ 55-14-09. Court proceedings.

(a) A dissolved corporation that has published a notice under G.S. 55-14-07 may file an application with the superior court of the county where the dissolved corporation's principal office, or its registered office if the corporation does not have a principal office in this State, is located for a determination of the amount and form of security to be provided for payments of claims that are contingent or have not been made known to the dissolved corporation or that are based on an event occurring after the effective date of dissolution but that, based on the facts known to the dissolved corporation, are reasonably estimated to arise after the effective date of dissolution. Provisions need not be made for any claim that is or is reasonably anticipated to be barred under G.S. 55-14-07(c).

(b) Within 10 days after the filing of the application, notice of the proceeding shall be given by the dissolved corporation to each claimant holding a contingent claim whose contingent claim is shown on the records of the dissolved corporation.

(c) The court may appoint a guardian ad litem to represent all claimants whose identities are unknown in any proceeding brought under this section. The reasonable fees and expenses of the guardian, including all reasonable expert witness fees, shall be paid by the dissolved corporation.

(d) Provision by the dissolved corporation for security in the amount and the form ordered by the court under subsection (a) of this section shall satisfy the dissolved corporation's obligations with respect to claims that are contingent, have not been made known to the dissolved corporation, or are based on an event occurring after the effective date of dissolution, and the claims shall not be enforced against a shareholder who received assets in liquidation. (2005-268, s. 33.)

§§ 55-14-10 through 55-14-19. Reserved for future codification purposes.

Part 2. Administrative Dissolution.

§ 55-14-20. Grounds for administrative dissolution.

The Secretary of State may commence a proceeding under G.S. 55-14-21 to dissolve administratively a corporation if:

(1) The corporation does not pay within 60 days after they are due any penalties, fees, or other payments due under this Chapter;

(2) The corporation is delinquent in delivering its annual report;

(3) The corporation is without a registered agent or registered office in this State for 60 days or more;

(4) The corporation does not notify the Secretary of State within 60 days that its registered agent or registered office has been changed, that its registered agent has resigned, or that its registered office has been discontinued;

(5) The corporation's period of duration stated in its articles of incorporation expires; or

(6) The corporation knowingly fails or refuses to answer truthfully and fully within the time prescribed in this Chapter interrogatories propounded by the Secretary of State in accordance with the provisions of this Chapter. (1989, c. 265, s. 1; 1993, c. 552, s. 15; 1997-475, s. 6.4.)

§ 55-14-21. Procedure for and effect of administrative dissolution.

(a) If the Secretary of State determines that one or more grounds exist under G.S. 55-14-20 for dissolving a corporation, he shall mail the corporation written notice of his determination.

(b) If the corporation does not correct each ground for dissolution or demonstrate to the reasonable satisfaction of the Secretary of State that each ground determined by the Secretary of State does not exist within 60 days after notice is mailed, the Secretary of State shall administratively dissolve the corporation by signing a certificate of dissolution that recites the ground or grounds for dissolution and its effective date. The Secretary of State shall file the original of the certificate and mail a copy to the corporation.

(c) The provisions of G.S. 55-14-05, 55-14-06, and 55-14-07 apply to a corporation administratively dissolved.

(d) The administrative dissolution of a corporation does not terminate the authority of its registered agent. (1989, c. 265, s. 1.)

§ 55-14-22. Reinstatement following administrative dissolution.

(a) A corporation administratively dissolved under G.S. 55-14-21 may apply to the Secretary of State for reinstatement. The application must:

(1) Recite the name of the corporation and the effective date of its administrative dissolution; and

(2) State that the ground or grounds for dissolution either did not exist or have been eliminated.

(3)   Reserved.

(4)   Repealed by Session Laws 1995, c. 539, s. 6.

(a1)   If, at the time the corporation applies for reinstatement, the name of the corporation is not distinguishable from the name of another entity authorized to be used under G.S. 55D-21, then the corporation must change its name to a name that is distinguishable upon the records of the Secretary of State from the name of the other entity before the Secretary of State may prepare a certificate of reinstatement.

(b)   If the Secretary of State determines that the application contains the information required by subsection (a) of this section, that the information is correct, and that the name of the corporation complies with G.S. 55D-21 and any other applicable section, the Secretary of State shall cancel the certificate of dissolution and prepare a certificate of reinstatement that recites the Secretary of State's determination and the effective date of reinstatement, file the original of the certificate, and mail a copy to the corporation.

(c)   When the reinstatement is effective, it relates back to and takes effect as of the date of the administrative dissolution and the corporation resumes carrying on its business as if the administrative dissolution had never occurred, subject to the rights of any person who reasonably relied to his prejudice upon the certificate of dissolution. (1989, c. 265, s. 1; 1995, c. 539, ss. 6, 7; 1996, 2nd Ex. Sess., c. 17, s. 15.1(b); 1997-200, ss. 1, 2(b); 1997-485, s. 1; 2001-390, s. 7; 2001-413, ss. 7, 7.1.)

§ 55-14-23. Appeal from denial of reinstatement.

(a)   If the Secretary of State denies a corporation's application for reinstatement following administrative dissolution, he shall serve the corporation under G.S. 55D-33 with a written notice that explains the reason or reasons for denial.

(b)   The corporation may appeal the denial of reinstatement to the Superior Court of Wake County within 30 days after service of the notice of denial is perfected. The appeal is commenced by filing a petition with the court and with the Secretary of State requesting the court to set aside the dissolution. The petition shall have attached to it copies of the Secretary of State's certificate of dissolution, the corporation's application for reinstatement, and the Secretary of State's notice of denial. No service of process on the Secretary of State is required except for the filing of the petition as set forth in this subsection. The appeal to the superior court shall be determined by a judge of the superior court upon such further evidence, notice and opportunity to be heard, if any, as the court may deem appropriate under the circumstances. The corporation shall have the burden of establishing that it is entitled to reinstatement.

(c) Upon consideration of the petition and any response made by the Secretary of State, the court may, prior to entering final judgment, order the Secretary of State to reinstate the dissolved corporation or may take other action the court considers appropriate.

(d) The court's final decision may be appealed as in other civil proceedings. (1989, c. 265, s. 1; 2001-358, ss. 5A(a), 47(d); 2001-387, ss. 173, 175(a); 2001-413, s. 6.)

§ 55-14-24. Inapplicability of Administrative Procedure Act.

The Administrative Procedure Act shall not apply to any proceeding or appeal provided for in G.S. 55-14-20 through 55-14-23. (1989, c. 265, s. 1.)

§§ 55-14-25 through 55-14-29. Reserved for future codification purposes.

Part 3. Judicial Dissolution.

§ 55-14-30. Grounds for judicial dissolution.

The superior court may dissolve a corporation:

(1) In a proceeding by the Attorney General if it is established that (i) the corporation obtained its articles of incorporation through fraud; or (ii) the corporation has, after written notice by the Attorney General given at least 20 days prior thereto, continued to exceed or abuse the authority conferred upon it by law;

(2)   In a proceeding by a shareholder if it is established that (i) the directors or those in control of the corporation are deadlocked in the management of the corporate affairs, the shareholders are unable to break the deadlock, and irreparable injury to the corporation is threatened or being suffered, or the business and affairs of the corporation can no longer be conducted to the advantage of the shareholders generally, because of the deadlock; (ii) liquidation is reasonably necessary for the protection of the rights or interests of the complaining shareholder; (iii) the shareholders are deadlocked in voting power and have failed, for a period that includes at least two consecutive annual meeting dates, to elect successors to directors whose terms have expired; (iv) the corporate assets are being misapplied or wasted; or (v) a written agreement, whether embodied in the articles of incorporation or separate therefrom, entitles the complaining shareholder to liquidation or dissolution of the corporation at will or upon the occurrence of some event which has subsequently occurred, and all present shareholders, and all subscribers and transferees of shares, either are parties to such agreement or became a shareholder, subscriber or transferee with actual notice thereof;

(3)   In a proceeding by a creditor if it is established that (i) the creditor's claim has been reduced to judgment and the execution on the judgment returned unsatisfied; or (ii) the corporation has admitted in writing that the creditor's claim is due and owing and the corporation is insolvent; or

(4)   In a proceeding by the corporation to have its voluntary dissolution continued under court supervision. (Code, ss. 604, 605, 619, 668, 669, 694; 1889, c. 533; 1901, c. 2, ss. 61, 62, 73; Rev., ss. 1196, 1198, 1203, 1204; C.S., ss. 1185, 1187, 1195; G.S., ss. 55-124, 55-126, 55-134; 1955, c. 1371, s. 1; 1959, c. 1316, s. 26; 1989, c. 265, s. 1.)

§ 55-14-31. Procedure for judicial dissolution.

(a)   Venue for a proceeding to dissolve a corporation lies in the county where a corporation's principal office (or, if none in this State, its registered office) is or was last located.

(b)   It is not necessary to make shareholders parties to a proceeding to dissolve a corporation unless relief is sought against them individually.

(c)   A court in a proceeding brought to dissolve a corporation may issue injunctions, appoint a receiver with all powers and duties the court directs, take other action required to preserve the corporate assets wherever located, and carry on the business of the corporation.

(d)   In any proceeding brought by a shareholder under G.S. 55-14-30(2)(ii) in which the court determines that dissolution would be appropriate, the court shall not order dissolution if, after such determination, the corporation elects to purchase the shares of the complaining shareholder at their fair value, as determined in accordance with such procedures as the court may provide. (1955, c. 1371, s. 1; 1959, c. 1316, s. 26; 1973, c. 469, s. 41; 1989, c. 265, s. 1.)

§ 55-14-32. Receivership.

(a)   A court in a judicial proceeding brought to dissolve a corporation may appoint one or more receivers to wind up and liquidate, or to manage, the business and affairs of the corporation. The court shall hold a hearing, after notifying all parties to the proceeding and any interested persons designated by the court, before appointing a receiver. The court appointing a receiver has exclusive jurisdiction over the corporation and all of its property wherever located.

(b)   The court may appoint an individual or a domestic or foreign corporation (authorized to transact business in this State) as a receiver. The court may require the receiver to post bond, with or without sureties, in an amount the court directs.

(c)   The court shall describe the powers and duties of the receiver in its appointing order, which may be amended from time to time. Such powers may include without limitation the power:

(1)   To dispose of all or any part of the assets of the corporation wherever located, at a public or private sale, if authorized by the court;

(1a)   To sue and defend in his own name as receiver of the corporation in all courts of this State; and

(2) To exercise all of the powers of the corporation, through or in place of its board of directors or officers, to the extent necessary to manage the affairs of the corporation in the best interests of its shareholders and creditors.

(d) Reserved for future codification purposes.

(e) The court from time to time during the receivership may order compensation paid and expense disbursements or reimbursements made to the receiver and his counsel from the assets of the corporation or proceeds from the sale of the assets. (1955, c. 1371, s. 1; 1989, c. 265, s. 1.)

§ 55-14-33. Decree of dissolution.

(a) If after a hearing the court determines that one or more grounds for judicial dissolution described in G.S. 55-14-30 exist, it may enter a decree dissolving the corporation and specifying the effective date of the dissolution, and the clerk of the court shall deliver a certified copy of the decree to the Secretary of State, who shall file it.

(b) After entering the decree of dissolution, the court shall direct the winding up and liquidation of the corporation's business and affairs in accordance with G.S. 55-14-05 and the notification of claimants in accordance with G.S. 55-14-06 and G.S. 55-14-07. The corporation's name becomes available for use by another entity as provided in G.S. 55D-21. (1955, c. 1371, s. 1; 1959, c. 1316, s. 26; 1967, c. 823, s. 19; 1969, c. 965, s. 1; 1973, c. 469, s. 42; 1989, c. 265, s. 1; 2001-358, s. 19; 2001-387, ss. 173, 175(a); 2001-413, s. 6.)

§§ 55-14-34 through 55-14-39. Reserved for future codification purposes.

Part 4. Miscellaneous.

§ 55-14-40. Disposition of amounts due to unavailable shareholders and creditors.

Upon liquidation of a corporation, the portion of the assets distributable to a creditor or shareholder who is unknown or cannot be found shall be disposed of in accordance with Chapter 116B. (1947, c. 613, c. 621, s. 1; G.S., s. 55-132; 1955, c. 1371, s. 1; 1971, c. 1135, s. 4; 1979 2nd Sess., c. 1311, s. 6; 1989, c. 265, s. 1.)

Article 14A.

Reorganization.

§ 55-14A-01. Fundamental changes in reorganization proceedings.

(a) Whenever a plan of reorganization of a corporation is confirmed by decree or order of a court of competent jurisdiction in proceedings for the reorganization of such corporation pursuant to the provisions of any applicable statute of the United States relating to reorganization of corporations, the corporation may put into effect and carry out such plan and the decrees and orders of the court relative thereto and may take any action provided in such plan or directed by such decrees and orders without further action by its directors or shareholders. Such action may be taken, as may be directed by such decrees or orders, by the trustee or trustees of such corporation appointed in the reorganization proceedings, or by designated officers of the corporation, or by a master or other representative appointed by the court, with like effect as if taken by unanimous action of the directors and shareholders of the corporation. In particular and without limiting the generality or effect of the foregoing, such corporation may:

(1) Amend its articles of incorporation or bylaws, or both, so long as the articles of incorporation and bylaws as amended contain only such provisions as might be lawfully contained therein at the time of making such amendment;

(2) Constitute or reconstitute and classify or reclassify its board of directors, and name, constitute or appoint directors and officers in place of or in addition to all or any of the directors or officers then in office;

(3) Make any change in its capital accounts or in any or all of its outstanding shares or other securities, or cancel any or all of such outstanding shares or other securities;

(4) Dissolve and liquidate;

(5) Effect a merger or share exchange;

(6) Transfer all or part of its assets;

(7) Change its registered office or registered agent, or both;

(8) Authorize the issuance of bonds, debentures or other obligations of the corporation, whether or not convertible into shares of any class or bearing warrants or other evidences of optional rights to purchase or subscribe for shares of any class, and fix the terms and conditions thereof.

(b) Any articles of amendment, statement of change of registered office or registered agent, articles of restatement, articles of merger or share exchange, articles of conversion, articles of dissolution, or any other document appropriate to complete any action permitted by this section shall be executed and filed in accordance with the provisions of this Chapter on behalf of the corporation by such person or persons as may be authorized to take such action pursuant to subsection (a) of this section. The document shall set forth the statements required by this Chapter to be included in the document, except any statement that the action taken by the document was adopted by the incorporators or board of directors or was approved by the shareholders, and also shall set forth:

(1) The date of the court's order or decree approving the action.

(2) The title of the reorganization proceeding in which the order or decree was entered.

(3) A statement that the court had jurisdiction of the proceeding under a federal statute of the United States.

(c) No action taken under this section shall give rise to any appraisal rights, except as provided in the plan of reorganization.

(d) This section does not apply after entry of a final decree in the reorganization proceeding even though the court retains jurisdiction of the proceeding for limited purposes unrelated to consummation of the reorganization plan. (1973, c. 469, s. 38; 1989, c. 265, s. 1; 2005-268, s. 34; 2011-347, s. 12.)

Article 15.

Foreign Corporations.

Part 1. Certificate of Authority.

§ 55-15-01. Authority to transact business required.

(a)   A foreign corporation may not transact business in this State until it obtains a certificate of authority from the Secretary of State.

(b)   Without excluding other activities which may not constitute transacting business in this State, a foreign corporation shall not be considered to be transacting business in this State solely for the purposes of this Chapter, by reason of carrying on in this State any one or more of the following activities:

(1)   Maintaining or defending any action or suit or any administrative or arbitration proceeding, or effecting the settlement thereof or the settlement of claims or disputes;

(2)   Holding meetings of its directors or shareholders or carrying on other activities concerning its internal affairs;

(3)   Maintaining bank accounts or borrowing money in this State, with or without security, even if such borrowings are repeated and continuous transactions;

(4)   Maintaining offices or agencies for the transfer, exchange, and registration of its securities, or appointing and maintaining trustees or depositories with relation to its securities;

(5)   Soliciting or procuring orders, whether by mail or through employees or agents or otherwise, where such orders require acceptance without this State before becoming binding contracts;

(6) Making or investing in loans with or without security including servicing of mortgages or deeds of trust through independent agencies within the State, the conducting of foreclosure proceedings and sale, the acquiring of property at foreclosure sale and the management and rental of such property for a reasonable time while liquidating its investment, provided no office or agency therefor is maintained in this State;

(7) Taking security for or collecting debts due to it or enforcing any rights in property securing the same;

(8) Transacting business in interstate commerce;

(9) Conducting an isolated transaction completed within a period of six months and not in the course of a number of repeated transactions of like nature;

(10) Selling through independent contractors;

(11) Owning, without more, real or personal property.

(c) Reserved for future codification purposes.

(d) Foreign insurance companies that are licensed by the Commissioner of Insurance are not required to obtain a certificate of authority from the Secretary of State. (1901, c. 2, s. 93; Rev., s. 1193; 1915, c. 196, s. 1; C.S., s. 1180; G.S., s. 55-117; 1955, c. 1371, s. 1; 1989, c. 265, s. 1; 1989 (Reg. Sess., 1990), c. 1024, s. 12.20; 1993, c. 552, s. 16.)

§ 55-15-02. Consequences of transacting business without authority.

(a) No foreign corporation transacting business in this State without permission obtained through a certificate of authority under this Chapter or through domestication under prior acts shall be permitted to maintain any action or proceeding in any court of this State unless the foreign corporation has obtained a certificate of authority prior to trial.

An issue arising under this subsection must be raised by motion and determined by the trial judge prior to trial.

(b) Reserved for future codification purposes.

(c) Reserved for future codification purposes.

(d) A foreign corporation failing to obtain a certificate of authority as required by this Chapter or by prior acts then applicable shall be liable to the State for the years or parts thereof during which it transacted business in this State without a certificate of authority in an amount equal to all fees and taxes which would have been imposed by law upon such corporation had it duly applied for and received such permission, plus interest and all penalties imposed by law for failure to pay such fees and taxes. In addition, the foreign corporation shall be liable for a civil penalty of ten dollars ($10.00) for each day, but not to exceed a total of one thousand dollars ($1,000) for each year or part thereof, it transacts business in this State without a certificate of authority. The Attorney General may bring actions to recover all amounts due the State under the provisions of this subsection.

The clear proceeds of civil penalties provided for in this subsection shall be remitted to the Civil Penalty and Forfeiture Fund in accordance with G.S. 115C-457.2.

(e) Notwithstanding subsection (a), the failure of a foreign corporation to obtain a certificate of authority does not impair the validity of its corporate acts or prevent it from defending any proceeding in this State.

(f) The Secretary of State is hereby directed to require that every foreign corporation transacting business in this State comply with the provisions of this Chapter. The Secretary of State is authorized to employ such assistants as shall be deemed necessary in his office for the purpose of enforcing the provisions of this Article and for making such investigations as shall be necessary to ascertain foreign corporations now transacting business in this State which may have failed to comply with the provisions of this Chapter. (1901, c. 2, s. 57; 1903, c. 76; Rev., s. 1194; 1915, c. 263; C.S., s. 1181; 1935, c. 44; 1937, c. 343; 1939, c. 57; G.S., ss. 55-118, 55-120; 1953, c. 1152; 1955, c. 1371, s. 1; 1989, c. 265, s. 1; 1998-215, s. 117; 1999-151, s. 1.)

§ 55-15-03. Application for certificate of authority.

(a) A foreign corporation may apply for a certificate of authority to transact business in this State by delivering an application to the Secretary of State for filing. The application must set forth:

(1) The name of the foreign corporation or, if its name is unavailable for use in this State, a corporate name that satisfies the requirements of Article 3 of Chapter 55D of the General Statutes;

(2) The name of the state or country under whose law it is incorporated;

(3) Its date of incorporation and period of duration;

(4) The street address, and the mailing address if different from the street address, of its principal office if any, and the county in which the principal office, if any, is located;

(5) The street address, and the mailing address if different from the street address, of its registered office in this State, the county in which the registered office is located, and the name of its registered agent at that office; and

(6) The names and usual business addresses of its current officers.

(b) The foreign corporation shall deliver with the completed application a certificate of existence (or a document of similar import) duly authenticated by the secretary of state or other official having custody of corporate records in the state or country under whose law it is incorporated.

(c) If the Secretary of State finds that the application conforms to law he shall, when all fees have been tendered as prescribed in this Chapter:

(1) Endorse on the application and an exact or conformed copy thereof the word "filed" and the hour, day, month, and year of the filing thereof;

(2) File in his office the application and the certificate of existence (or document of similar import as described in subsection (b) of this section);

(3) Issue a certificate of authority to transact business in this State to which he shall affix the exact or conformed copy of the application; and

(4) Send to the foreign corporation or its representative the certificate of authority, together with the exact or conformed copy of the application affixed

thereto. (1901, c. 2, s. 57; 1903, c. 766; Rev., s. 1194; 1915, c. 263; C.S., s. 1181; 1935, c. 44; 1939, c. 57; G.S., s. 55-118; 1953, c. 1152; 1955, c. 1371, s. 1; 1957, c. 979, s. 8; 1969, c. 751, s. 41; 1989, c. 265, s. 1; 1989 (Reg. Sess., 1990), c. 1024, ss. 12.1(b), 12.21; 2001-358, s. 17; 2001-387, ss. 27A, 169(a), 173, 175(a); 2001-413, s. 6.)

§ 55-15-04. Amended certificate of authority.

(a) A foreign corporation authorized to transact business in this State must obtain an amended certificate of authority from the Secretary of State if it changes:

(1) Its corporate name;

(2) The period of its duration; or

(3) The state or country of its incorporation.

(b) A foreign corporation may apply for an amended certificate of authority by delivering an application to the Secretary of State for filing that sets forth:

(1) The name of the foreign corporation and the name in which the corporation is authorized to transact business in North Carolina if different;

(2) The name of the state or country under whose law it is incorporated;

(3) The date it was originally authorized to transact business in this State;

(4) A statement of the change or changes being made.

Except for the content of the application, the requirements of G.S. 55-15-03 for obtaining an original certificate of authority apply to obtaining an amended certificate under this section. (1955, c. 1371, s. 1; 1989, c. 265, s. 1; 1989 (Reg. Sess., 1990), c. 1024, s. 12.22.)

§ 55-15-05. Effect of certificate of authority.

(a)   A certificate of authority authorizes the foreign corporation to which it is issued to transact business in this State subject, however, to the right of the State to revoke the certificate as provided in this Chapter. A foreign corporation may qualify in this State as executor, administrator, or guardian, or as trustee under the will of any person domiciled in this State at the time of that person's death only in accordance with applicable provisions of Article 24 of Chapter 53.

A foreign corporation qualifying as testamentary trustee or executor under the provisions of this section shall appoint a process agent and file such appointment with the court as required by G.S. 28A-4-2(4).

(b)   Except as otherwise provided by this Chapter, a foreign corporation with a valid certificate of authority has the same but no greater rights and has the same but no greater privileges as, and is subject to the same duties, restrictions, penalties, and liabilities now or later imposed on, a domestic corporation of like character.

(c)   Reserved for future codification purposes. (1901, c. 2, s. 93; Rev., s. 1193; 1915, c. 196, s. 1; C.S., s. 1180; G.S., s. 55-117; 1955, c. 1371, s. 1; 1969, c. 839; 1985, c. 689, s. 25; 1989, c. 265, s. 1; 2001-263, s. 4.)

§ 55-15-06: Repealed by Session Laws 2001-358, s. 18.

§ 55-15-07. Registered office and registered agent of foreign corporation.

Each foreign corporation authorized to transact business in this State must maintain a registered office and registered agent as required by Article 4 of Chapter 55D of the General Statutes and is subject to service on the Secretary of State under that Article. (1901, c. 5; Rev., s. 1243; C.S., s. 1137; G.S., s. 55-38; 1955, c. 1371, s. 1; 1989, c. 265, s. 1; 2000-140, s. 101(c); 2001-358, s. 47(b); 2001-387, ss. 173, 175(a); 2001-413, s. 6.)

§§ 55-15-08 through 55-15-10: Repealed by Session Laws 2001-358, s. 47(c), effective January 1, 2002.

§§ 55-15-11 through 55-15-19. Reserved for future codification purposes.

Part 2. Withdrawal.

§ 55-15-20. Withdrawal of foreign corporation.

(a) A foreign corporation authorized to transact business in this State may not withdraw from this State until it obtains a certificate of withdrawal from the Secretary of State.

(b) A foreign corporation authorized to transact business in this State may apply for a certificate of withdrawal by delivering an application to the Secretary of State for filing. The application must set forth:

(1) The name of the foreign corporation and the name of the state or country under whose law it is incorporated;

(2) That it is not transacting business in this State and that it surrenders its authority to transact business in this State;

(3) That the corporation revokes the authority of its registered agent to accept service of process and consents that service of process in any action or proceeding based upon any cause of action arising in this State, or arising out of business transacted in this State, during the time the corporation was authorized to transact business in this State may thereafter be made on such corporation by service thereof on the Secretary of State;

(4) A mailing address to which the Secretary of State may mail a copy of any process served on the Secretary of State under subdivision (3); and

(5) A commitment to file with the Secretary of State a statement of any subsequent change in its mailing address.

(b1) If the Secretary of State finds that such application conforms to law, he shall:

(1)   Endorse on the application and an exact or conformed copy thereof the word "filed", and the hour, day, month and year of the filing thereof;

(2)   File the application in his office;

(3)   Issue a certificate of withdrawal to which he shall affix the exact or conformed copy of the application; and

(4)   Send to the foreign corporation or its representative the certificate of withdrawal together with the exact or conformed copy of the application affixed thereto.

(c)   After the withdrawal of the foreign corporation is effective, service of process on the Secretary of State in accordance with subsection (b) of this section shall be made by delivering to and leaving with the Secretary of State, or with any clerk authorized by the Secretary of State to accept service of process, duplicate copies of the process and the fee required by G.S. 55-1-22(b). Upon receipt of process in the manner provided in this subsection, the Secretary of State shall immediately mail a copy of the process by registered or certified mail, return receipt requested, to the foreign corporation at the mailing address designated pursuant to subsection (b) of this section. (1955, c. 1371, s. 1; 1973, c. 476, s. 193; 1989, c. 265, s. 1; 1989 (Reg. Sess., 1990), c. 1024, s. 12.23; 2001-387, ss. 29, 30.)

§ 55-15-21. Withdrawal of foreign corporation by reason of a merger, consolidation, or conversion.

(a)   Whenever a foreign corporation authorized to transact business in this State ceases its separate existence as a result of a statutory merger or consolidation permitted by the laws of the state or country under which it was incorporated, or converts into another entity as permitted by those laws, the surviving or resulting entity shall apply for a certificate of withdrawal for the foreign corporation by delivering to the Secretary of State for filing a copy of the articles of merger, consolidation, or conversion or a certificate reciting the facts of the merger, consolidation, or conversion, duly authenticated by the Secretary of State or other official having custody of corporate records in the state or country under the laws of which such foreign corporation was incorporated. If the surviving or resulting entity is not authorized to transact business or conduct affairs in this State the articles or certificate must be accompanied by an application that sets forth:

(1)   The name of the foreign corporation authorized to transact business in this State, the type of entity and name of the surviving or resulting entity, and a statement that the surviving or resulting entity is not authorized to transact business or conduct affairs in this State;

(2)   A statement that the surviving or resulting entity consents that service of process based upon any cause of action arising in this State, or arising out of business transacted in this State, during the time the foreign corporation was authorized to transact business in this State may thereafter be made by service thereof on the Secretary of State;

(3)   A mailing address to which the Secretary of State may mail a copy of any process served on the Secretary of State under subdivision (a)(2) of this section; and

(4)   A commitment to file with the Secretary of State a statement of any subsequent change in its mailing address.

(b)   If the Secretary of State finds that the articles or certificate and the application for withdrawal, if required, conform to law the Secretary of State shall:

(1)   Endorse on the articles or certificate and the application for withdrawal, if required, the word "filed" and the hour, day, month and year of the filing thereof;

(2)   File the articles or certificate and the application, if required;

(3)   Issue a certificate of withdrawal; and

(4)   Send to the surviving or resulting entity or its representative the certificate of withdrawal, together with the exact or conformed copy of the application, if required, affixed thereto.

(c)   After the withdrawal of the foreign corporation is effective, service of process on the Secretary of State in accordance with subsection (a) of this section shall be made by delivering to and leaving with the Secretary of State, or with any clerk authorized by the Secretary of State to accept service of process, duplicate copies of the process and the fee required by G.S. 55-1-22(b). Upon receipt of process in the manner provided in this subsection, the Secretary of State shall immediately mail a copy of the process by registered or certified mail, return receipt requested, to the surviving or resulting entity at the mailing address designated pursuant to subsection (a) of this section. (1991, c. 645, s. 13; 1999-369, s. 1.9; 2001-387, s. 31.)

§§ 55-15-22 through 55-15-29. Reserved for future codification purposes.

Part 3. Revocation of Certificate of Authority.

§ 55-15-30. Grounds for revocation.

(a) The Secretary of State may commence a proceeding under G.S. 55-15-31 to revoke the certificate of authority of a foreign corporation authorized to transact business in this State if:

(1) The foreign corporation is delinquent in delivering its annual report;

(2) The foreign corporation does not pay within 60 days after they are due any penalties, fees, or other payments due under this Chapter;

(3) The foreign corporation is without a registered agent or registered office in this State for 60 days or more;

(4) The foreign corporation does not inform the Secretary of State under G.S. 55D-31 or G.S. 55D-32 that its registered agent or registered office has changed, that its registered agent has resigned, or that its registered office has been discontinued within 60 days of the change, resignation, or discontinuance;

(5) An incorporator, director, officer, or agent of the foreign corporation signed a document he knew was false in any material respect with intent that the document be delivered to the Secretary of State for filing;

(6) The Secretary of State receives a duly authenticated certificate from the secretary of state or other official having custody of corporate records in the

state or country under whose law the foreign corporation is incorporated stating that it has been dissolved or disappeared as the result of a merger;

(7)   The corporation is exceeding the authority conferred upon it by this Chapter; or

(8)   The corporation knowingly fails or refuses to answer truthfully and fully within the time prescribed in this Chapter interrogatories propounded by the Secretary of State in accordance with the provisions of this Chapter.

(b)   Nothing herein shall be deemed to repeal or modify any provision of the Revenue Act relating to the suspension of the certificate of authority of foreign corporations for failure to comply with the provisions thereof. (1955, c. 1371, s. 1; 1989, c. 265, s. 1; 1993, c. 552, s. 18; 1997-475, s. 6.5; 2001-358, s. 47(e); 2001-387, ss. 173, 175(a); 2001-413, s. 6.)

§ 55-15-31. Procedure for and effect of revocation.

(a)   If the Secretary of State determines that one or more grounds exist under G.S. 55-15-30 for revocation of a certificate of authority, he shall mail to the foreign corporation written notice of his determination.

(b)   If the foreign corporation does not correct each ground for revocation or demonstrate to the reasonable satisfaction of the Secretary of State that each ground determined by the Secretary of State does not exist within 60 days after notice is mailed, the Secretary of State may revoke the foreign corporation's certificate of authority by signing a certificate of revocation that recites the ground or grounds for revocation and its effective date. The Secretary of State shall file the original of the certificate and mail a copy to the foreign corporation.

(c)   The authority of a foreign corporation to transact business in this State ceases on the date shown on the certificate revoking its certificate of authority.

(d)   The Secretary of State's revocation of a foreign corporation's certificate of authority appoints the Secretary of State the foreign corporation's agent for service of process in any proceeding based on a cause of action arising in this State or arising out of business transacted in this State during the time the foreign corporation was authorized to transact business in this State. The Secretary of State shall then proceed in accordance with G.S. 55D-33.

(e) Revocation of a foreign corporation's certificate of authority does not terminate the authority of the registered agent of the corporation.

(f) The corporation shall not be granted a new certificate of authority until each ground for revocation has been substantially corrected to the reasonable satisfaction of the Secretary of State. (1955, c. 1371, s. 1; 1989, c. 265, s. 1; 1989 (Reg. Sess., 1990), c. 1024, s. 12.24; 1991, c. 645, s. 14; 2001-358, s. 47(f); 2001-387, ss. 173, 175(a); 2001-413, s. 6.)

§ 55-15-32. Appeal from revocation.

(a) A foreign corporation may appeal the Secretary of State's revocation of its certificate of authority to the Superior Court of Wake County within 30 days after the certificate of revocation is mailed to the foreign corporation by the Secretary of State. The appeal is commenced by filing a petition with the court and with the Secretary of State requesting the court to set aside the revocation. The petition shall have attached to it copies of the corporation's certificate of authority and the Secretary of State's certificate of revocation. No service of process on the Secretary of State is required except for the filing of the petition as set forth in this subsection. The appeal to the superior court shall be determined by a judge of the superior court upon such further evidence, notice and opportunity to be heard, if any, as the court may deem appropriate under the circumstances. The foreign corporation shall have the burden of establishing that it is entitled to have the revocation set aside.

(b) Upon consideration of the petition and any response made by the Secretary of State, the court may, prior to entering final judgment, order the Secretary of State to set aside the revocation or may take any other action the court considers appropriate.

(c) The court's final decision may be appealed as in other civil proceedings. (1989, c. 265, s. 1; 1989 (Reg. Sess., 1990), c. 1024, s. 12.25; 2001-358, s. 5A(b); 2001-387, ss. 173, 175(a); 2001-413, s. 6.)

§ 55-15-33. Inapplicability of Administrative Procedure Act.

The Administrative Procedure Act shall not apply to any proceeding or appeal provided for in G.S. 55-15-30 through 55-15-32. (1989, c. 265, s. 1.)

Article 16.

Records and Reports.

Part 1. Records.

§ 55-16-01. Corporate records.

(a) A corporation shall keep as permanent records minutes of all meetings of its incorporators, shareholders and board of directors, a record of all actions taken by the shareholders or board of directors without a meeting, and a record of all actions taken by a committee of the board of directors in place of the board of directors on behalf of the corporation.

(b) A corporation shall maintain appropriate accounting records.

(c) A corporation or its agent shall maintain a record of its shareholders, in a form that permits preparation of a list of the names and addresses of all shareholders, in alphabetical order by class of shares showing the number and class of shares held by each.

(d) A corporation shall maintain its records in written form or in another form capable of conversion into written form within a reasonable time.

(e) A corporation shall keep a copy of the following records at its principal office:

(1) Its articles or restated articles of incorporation and all amendments to them currently in effect;

(2) Its bylaws or restated bylaws and all amendments to them currently in effect;

(3) Resolutions adopted by its board of directors creating one or more classes or series of shares, and fixing their relative rights, preferences, and limitations, if shares issued pursuant to those resolutions are outstanding;

(4) The minutes of all shareholders' meetings, and records of all action taken by shareholders without a meeting, for the past three years;

(5) All written communications to shareholders generally within the past three years and the financial statements required to be made available to the shareholders for the past three years under G.S. 55-16-20;

(6) A list of the names and business addresses of its current directors and officers; and

(7) Its most recent annual report delivered as required by G.S. 55-16-22. (1901, c. 2, ss. 38, 45; Rev., ss. 1180, 1181; C.S., s. 1170; G.S., s. 55-107; 1955, c. 1371, s. 1; 1969, c. 751, s. 14; 1989, c. 265, s. 1; 1997-475, s. 6.6.)

§ 55-16-02. Inspection of records by shareholders.

(a) A qualified shareholder of a corporation is entitled to inspect and copy, during regular business hours at the corporation's principal office, any of the records of the corporation described in G.S. 55-16-01(e) if he gives the corporation written notice of his demand at least five business days before the date on which he wishes to inspect and copy.

(b) A qualified shareholder of a corporation is entitled to inspect and copy, during regular business hours at a reasonable location specified by the corporation, any of the following records of the corporation if the shareholder meets the requirements of subsection (c) and gives the corporation written notice of his demand at least five business days before the date on which he wishes to inspect and copy:

(1) Records of any final action taken with or without a meeting by the board of directors, or by a committee of the board of directors while acting in place of the board of directors on behalf of the corporation, minutes of any meeting of the shareholders and records of action taken by the shareholders without a meeting, to the extent not subject to inspection under G.S. 55-16-02 (a);

(2) Accounting records of the corporation; and

(3) The record of shareholders;

provided that a shareholder of a public corporation shall not be entitled to inspect or copy any accounting records of the corporation or any records of the corporation with respect to any matter which the corporation determines in good faith may, if disclosed, adversely affect the corporation in the conduct of its business or may constitute material nonpublic information at the time the shareholder's notice of demand to inspect and copy is received by the corporation.

(c) A qualified shareholder may inspect and copy the records described in subsection (b) only if:

(1) His demand is made in good faith and for a proper purpose;

(2) He describes with reasonable particularity his purpose and the records he desires to inspect; and

(3) The records are directly connected with his purpose.

(d) The right of inspection granted by this section may not be abolished or limited by a corporation's articles of incorporation or bylaws.

(e) This section does not affect:

(1) The right of a shareholder to inspect records under G.S. 55-7-20 or, if the shareholder is in litigation with the corporation, to inspect the records to the same extent as any other litigant;

(2) The power of a court, independently of this Chapter, to compel the production of corporate records for examination.

(f) For purposes of this section, "shareholder" includes a beneficial owner whose shares are held in a voting trust or by a nominee on his behalf and whose beneficial ownership is certified to the corporation by that voting trust or nominee.

(g) For purposes of this section a "qualified shareholder" of a corporation is a person who shall have been a shareholder in the corporation for at least six months immediately preceding his demand or who shall be the holder of at least five percent (5%) of the corporation's outstanding shares of any class.

(h) A qualified shareholder of a corporation that has the power to elect, appoint, or designate a majority of the directors of another domestic or foreign corporation or of a domestic or foreign nonprofit corporation, shall have the inspection rights provided in this section with respect to the records of that other corporation.

(i) Notwithstanding the provisions of this section or any other provisions of this Chapter or interpretations thereof to the contrary, a shareholder of a public corporation shall have no common law rights to inspect or copy any accounting records of the corporation or any other records of the corporation that may not be inspected or copied by a shareholder of a public corporation as provided in G.S. 55-16-02(b). (1901, c. 2, ss. 38, 45, 49; Rev., ss. 1179-1181; C.S., ss. 1170, 1172; G.S., ss. 55-107, 55-109; 1955, c. 1371, s. 1; 1965, c. 609; 1973, c. 469, s. 11; 1989, c. 265, s. 1; 1989 (Reg. Sess., 1990), c. 1024, s. 12.26; 1993, c. 552, s. 19.)

§ 55-16-03. Scope of inspection right.

(a) A shareholder's agent or attorney has the same inspection and copying rights as the shareholder represented.

(b) The right to copy records under G.S. 55-16-02 includes, if reasonable, the right to receive copies by xerographic or other means, including copies through an electronic transmission if available and so requested by the shareholder.

(c) The corporation may impose a reasonable charge, covering the costs of labor and material, for producing for inspection or copying any records provided to the shareholder. The charge may not exceed the estimated cost of production, reproduction, or transmission of the records.

(d) The corporation may comply with a shareholder's demand to inspect the record of shareholders under G.S. 55-16-02(b)(3) by providing the shareholder with a list of its shareholders that was compiled no earlier than the date of the shareholder's demand. (1901, c. 2, s. 49; Rev., s. 1179; C.S., s. 1172; G.S., s.

55-109; 1955, c. 1371, s. 1; 1965, c. 609; 1973, c. 469, s. 11; 1989, c. 265, s. 1; 2005-268, s. 35.)

§ 55-16-04. Court-ordered inspection.

(a) If a corporation does not allow a shareholder who complies with G.S. 55-16-02(a) to inspect and copy any records required by that subsection to be available for inspection, the superior court of the county where the corporation's principal office (or, if none in this State, its registered office) is located may, upon application of the shareholder, summarily order inspection and copying of the records demanded at the corporation's expense.

(b) If a corporation does not within a reasonable time allow a shareholder to inspect and copy any other record, the shareholder who complies with G.S. 55-16-02(b) and (c) may apply to the superior court in the county where the corporation's principal office (or, if none in this State, its registered office) is located for an order to permit inspection and copying of the records demanded. The court shall dispose of an application under this subsection on an expedited basis.

(c) If the court orders inspection and copying of the records demanded, it shall also order the corporation to pay the shareholder's costs (including reasonable attorneys' fees) incurred to obtain the order unless the corporation proves that it refused inspection in good faith because it had a reasonable basis for doubt about the right of the shareholder to inspect the records demanded.

(d) If the court orders inspection and copying of the records demanded, it may impose reasonable restrictions on the use or distribution of the records by the demanding shareholder. (1901, c. 2, s. 49; Rev., s. 1179, C.S., s. 1172; G.S., s. 55-109; 1955, c. 1371, s. 1; 1965, c. 609; 1973, c. 469, s. 11; 1989, c. 265, s. 1.)

§ 55-16-05. Inspection of records by directors.

(a) A director of a corporation is entitled to inspect and copy the books, records, and documents of the corporation at any reasonable time to the extent reasonably related to the performance of the director's duties as a director, including duties as a member of a committee, but not for any other purpose or in any manner that would violate any duty to the corporation.

(b) The superior court of the county where the corporation's principal office, or its registered office if the corporation does not have a principal office in this State, is located may order inspection and copying of the books, records, and documents at the corporation's expense, upon application of a director who has been refused inspection rights, unless the corporation establishes that the director is not entitled to inspection rights. The court shall dispose of an application under this subsection on an expedited basis.

(c) If an order is issued, the court may include provisions protecting the corporation from undue burden or expense, and prohibiting the director from using information obtained upon exercise of the inspection rights in a manner that would violate a duty to the corporation, and may also order the corporation to reimburse the director for the director's costs, including reasonable counsel fees, incurred in connection with the application. (2005-268, s. 36.)

§ 55-16-06. Exception to notice requirements.

(a) Whenever notice is required to be given under any provision of this Chapter to a shareholder, the notice shall not be required to be given if either of the following applies:

(1) Notice of two consecutive annual meetings, and all notices of meetings during the period between those two consecutive annual meetings, have been sent to the shareholder at the shareholder's address as shown on the records of the corporation and have been returned undeliverable.

(2) All, but not less than two, payments of dividends on securities during a 12-month period, or two consecutive payments of dividends on securities during a period of more than 12 months, have been sent to the shareholder at the shareholder's address as shown on the records of the corporation and have been returned undeliverable.

(b) If a shareholder delivers to the corporation a written notice setting forth that shareholder's current address, the requirement that notice be given to the shareholder shall be reinstated. (2005-268, s. 36.)

§§ 55-16-07 through 55-16-19. Reserved for future codification purposes.

Part 2. Reports.

§ 55-16-20. Financial statements for shareholders.

(a) A corporation shall make available to its shareholders annual financial statements, which may be consolidated or combined statements of the corporation and one or more of its subsidiaries, as appropriate, that include a balance sheet as of the end of the fiscal year, an income statement for that year, and a statement of cash flows for the year unless that information appears elsewhere in the financial statements. If financial statements are prepared for the corporation on the basis of generally accepted accounting principles, the annual financial statements must also be prepared on that basis.

(b) If the annual financial statements are reported upon by a public accountant, his report must accompany them. If not, the statements must be accompanied by a statement of the president or the person responsible for the corporation's accounting records:

(1) Stating his reasonable belief whether the statements were prepared on the basis of generally accepted accounting principles and, if not, describing the basis of preparation; and

(2) Describing any respects in which the statements were not prepared on a basis of accounting consistent with the statements prepared for the preceding year.

(c) A corporation shall mail the annual financial statements, or a written notice of their availability, to each shareholder within 120 days after the close of each fiscal year; provided that the failure of the corporation to comply with this requirement shall not constitute the basis for any claim of damages by any shareholder unless such failure was in bad faith. Thereafter, on written request from a shareholder who was not mailed the statements, the corporation shall mail him the latest financial statements. (1901, c. 2, ss. 38, 45, 49; Rev., ss. 1179-1181; C.S., ss. 1170, 1172; G.S., ss. 55-107, 55-109; 1955, c. 1371, s. 1; 1965, c. 609; 1973, c. 469, s. 11; 1989, c. 265, s. 1.)

§ 55-16-21: Repealed by Session Laws 2005-268, s. 37, effective October 1, 2005.

§ 55-16-22. Annual report.

(a) Except as provided in subsections (a1) and (a2) of this section, each domestic corporation and each foreign corporation authorized to transact business in this State shall deliver an annual report to the Secretary of Revenue in paper form or, in the alternative, directly to the Secretary of State in electronic form as prescribed by the Secretary of State under this section.

(a1) Each insurance company subject to the provisions of Chapter 58 of the General Statutes shall deliver an annual report to the Secretary of State.

(a2) A domestic corporation governed by Chapter 55B of the General Statutes is exempt from this section.

(a3) The annual report required by this section shall be in a form jointly prescribed by the Secretary of Revenue and the Secretary of State. The Secretary of Revenue shall provide the form needed to file an annual report. The Secretary of State shall prescribe the form needed to file an annual report electronically and shall provide this form by electronic means. The annual report shall set forth all of the following:

(1) The name of the corporation and the state or country under whose law it is incorporated.

(2) The street address, and the mailing address if different from the street address, of the registered office, the county in which its registered office is located, and the name of its registered agent at that office in this State, and a statement of any change of such registered office or registered agent, or both.

(3) The address and telephone number of its principal office.

(4) The names, titles, and business addresses of its principal officers.

(4a) Repealed by Session Laws 1997-475, s. 6.1, effective January 1, 1998.

(5) A brief description of the nature of its business.

If the information contained in the most recently filed annual report has not changed, a certification to that effect may be made instead of setting forth the information required by subdivisions (2) through (5) of this subsection.

(b) Information in the annual report must be current as of the date the annual report is executed on behalf of the corporation.

(c) Due Date. - An annual report eligible to be delivered to the Secretary of Revenue is due by the due date for filing the corporation's income and franchise tax returns. An extension of time to file a return is an extension of time to file an annual report. At the option of the filer, an annual report may be filed directly with the Secretary of State in electronic form. An annual report required to be delivered to the Secretary of State is due by the fifteenth day of the fourth month following the close of the corporation's fiscal year.

(d) If an annual report does not contain the information required by this section, the Secretary of State shall promptly notify the reporting domestic or foreign corporation in writing and return the report to it for correction. If the report is corrected to contain the information required by this section and delivered to the Secretary of State within 30 days after the effective date of notice, it is deemed to be timely filed.

(e) Amendments to any previously filed annual report may be filed with the Secretary of State at any time for the purpose of correcting, updating, or augmenting the information contained in the annual report.

(f) Expired.

(g) When a statement of change of registered office or registered agent is filed in the annual report, the change shall become effective when the statement is received by the Secretary of State.

(h) If the Secretary of State does not receive an annual report within 120 days of the date the return is due, the Secretary of State may presume that the annual report is delinquent. This presumption may be rebutted by receipt of the annual report from the Secretary of Revenue or by evidence of delivery presented by the filing corporation. (1989, c. 265, s. 1; 1989 (Reg. Sess.,

1990), c. 1066, s. 32(a); 1993, c. 218, s. 2; 1997-475, s. 6.1; 2003-233, s. 3; 2010-31, s. 31.4(a).)

§ 55-16-22.1. Repealed by Session Laws 1998-228, S.17.

Article 17.

Transition and Curative Provisions.

§ 55-17-01. Applicability of act.

(a) The provisions of this Chapter shall apply to every corporation for profit, and, so far as appropriate, to every corporation not for profit having a capital stock, now existing or hereafter formed, and to the outstanding and future securities thereof, except to the extent the corporation is expressly excepted by this Chapter from its operation or except to the extent that there is other specific statutory provision particularly applicable to the corporation or inconsistent with some provisions of this Chapter, in which case that other provision prevails.

(b) Notwithstanding the provisions of subsection (a) of this section, no corporation not for profit having a capital stock and formed for religious, charitable, nonprofit, social, or literary purposes shall hereafter be formed under this Chapter. (1955, c. 1371, s. 1; 1957, c. 550, s. 1; 1973, c. 469, s. 1; 1989, c. 265, s. 1.)

§ 55-17-02. Application to qualified foreign corporations.

A foreign corporation authorized to transact business in this State on July 1, 1990 is subject to this Chapter but is not required to obtain a new certificate of authority to transact business under this Chapter. (1955, c. 1371, s. 1; 1957, c. 979, ss. 18, 19; 1989, c. 265, s. 1.)

§ 55-17-03. Saving provisions.

(a) The existence of corporations formed before July 1, 1990, shall not be impaired by the enactment of this Chapter nor by any change made by this Chapter in the requirements for the formation of corporations nor by any amendment or repeal by this Chapter of the laws under which they were formed or created, and, except as otherwise expressly provided in this Chapter, the repeal of a prior act by this Chapter shall not affect any liability or penalty incurred, under the provisions of such act, prior to the repeal thereof.

(b) Any proceeding or corporate action commenced before July 1, 1990, may be completed in accordance with the law then in effect.

(c) A corporation dissolved by operation of law before July 1, 1990, may wind up and liquidate its business and affairs pursuant to the provisions of Article 14 of this Chapter. (1955, c. 1371, s. 1; 1957, c. 550, s. 1; 1973, c. 469, s. 1; 1989, c. 265, s. 1; 1993, c. 218, s. 1.)

§ 55-17-04. Severability.

If any provision of this Chapter or its application to any person or circumstance is held invalid by a court of competent jurisdiction, the invalidity does not affect other provisions or applications of the Chapter that can be given effect without the invalid provision or application, and to this end the provisions of the Chapter are severable. (1989, c. 265, s. 1.)

§ 55-17-05. Curative statute.

All deeds, conveyances and other instruments executed prior to the effective date of this Chapter and validated by the curative provisions of former G.S. 55-36.1 and former Article 12 of Chapter 55 as they were immediately prior to such effective date shall be valid and effective to the same extent as if those provisions had not been amended or repealed. The provisions of former G.S. 55-36 shall continue to apply to all instruments executed before July 1, 1990, to which that section applied. (1905, c. 316; Rev., s. 1248; 1939, c. 23; 1941, c. 294; 1943, c. 219, s. 1 1/2; 1947, c. 504, ss. 1, 2; 1949, c. 436; c. 825; 1951, c. 395; C.S., s. 1134; G.S., ss. 55-35, 55-41, 55-41.1, 55-41.2, 55-42, 55-164.1,

55-164.2; 1955, c. 1371, s. 2; 1957, c. 500, s. 2; 1969, c. 953, s. 1; 1971, c. 60; 1977, c. 40, s. 1; 1979, c. 364; 1989, c. 265, s. 1; 1991, c. 647, s. 1.)

Vision Books Order Form

Fax Orders:	1-980-299-5965
Phone Orders:	1-704-898-0770
E-mail Orders:	www.visionbooks.org
Mail Orders:	Vision Books, LLC P.O. Box 42406 Charlotte, NC 28215

Shipp To:
Name_____
Address_____
City_____ State_____ Zip_____
Phone_____ Fax_____
Email_____ @_____

Bill To: We can bill a third party on your behalf.
Name_____
Address_____
City_____ State_____ Zip_____
Phone____(_____)_____ Fax_____
Email_____ @_____

Pamphlet Number ($15.00 Each)	Qty	Total Cost
_____	_____	_____
_____	_____	_____
_____	_____	_____
_____	_____	_____
_____	_____	_____
_____	_____	_____
_____	_____	_____
_____	_____	_____
Full Volume Set 1-92	**92 Pamphlets**	**1,380.00**

Free Shipping Shipping & Handling on Full Volume Orders
Add $1.00 Shipping & Handling per pamphlet $_____

Total Cost $_____

Thank you for your support. Management!

DID YOU ENJOY THIS BOOK?

Vision Books, LLC would like to hear from you! If you or someone you know has been fasely imprisoned, we would like to hear your story. If the 'North Carolina Criminal Law and Procedure' has had an effect in your life or if you have suggestions, we would like to hear from you. Send your letters to:

Vision Books, LLC
Attn: Staff Writers
P.O. Box 42406
Charlotte, NC 28215
Email: staff@visionbooks.org

Order Additional Copies:

Fax Orders:			1-980-299-5965

Phone Orders:		1-704-898-0770

E-mail Orders:		www.visionbooks.org

Mail Orders:		Vision Books, LLC
			P.O. Box 42406
			Charlotte, NC 28215

www.ingramcontent.com/pod-product-compliance
Lightning Source LLC
Chambersburg PA
CBHW051644170526
45167CB00001B/329